L.B.S.H.
Return

# The Hero Journey in Dreams

The
Hero Journey
in Dreams

# The Hero Journey in Dreams

JEAN DALBY CLIFT
and WALLACE B. CLIFT

CROSSROAD • NEW YORK

**1988**

The Crossroad Publishing Company
370 Lexington Avenue, New York, N.Y. 10017

Copyright © 1988 by Jean Dalby Clift and Wallace B. Clift

All rights reserved. No part of this book may be reproduced, stored in a retrieval system, or transmitted, in any form or by any means, electronic, mechanical, photocopying, recording or otherwise, without the written permission of The Crossroad Publishing Company.

Printed in the United States of America

*Library of Congress Cataloging-in-Publication Data*

Clift, Jean Dalby.
  The hero journey in dreams.

  Includes index.
  1. Dreams.  2. Heroes.  I. Clift, Wallace B.
II. Title.
BF1099.H47C57   1988     154.6'34     88-18917
ISBN 0-8245-0889-0

*For our grandchildren*
*Sarah*
*Evan*
*Dylan*
*David*
*and those yet to come*
*with our hopes for courage in*
*their hero journeys*

# Contents

*Introduction* ix

**Part I | The Pattern of Life's Journey** 1

1 • Living a Story   3
2 • The Monomyth   13
3 • The Human Journey   21
4 • Gender and Journey   29
5 • Understanding Dreams   37

**Part II | Hero Motifs in Dreams** 43

6 • The Call to Adventure   45
7 • Crossing the Threshold   61
8 • Discernment: Helpers or Tempters   76
9 • The Road of Trials   90
10 • Rites of Passage   108
11 • The Return   126

**Part III | Dream Series** 143

12 • Dreams and Suicide   145
13 • A Repeated Symbol   154
14 • A Monk's Dreams   163
15 • A Nun's Dreams   173
16 • Prayer and Active Imagination   183

*Afterword* 191
*Appendix: Exercises for Reflection* 195
*Notes* 199
*Index* 207

# Introduction

The hero gets a lot of attention nowadays. From the fictional antiheroes of recent decades to the current agonizing over the loss of the idealism of the American frontier, the issue of the hero is often raised. There seems to be something basic for the human spirit in the idea of the hero.

Is the focus on the heroic ideal out of date? Has the time for individualism ended? Does the heroic stance militate against peace for the world? Are women ever heroes? Is the "feminine" antithetical to the hero journey? Can one be truly "spiritual" if one is a hero?

In effect, all these questions raise the central issue of the *meaning* of the ancient pattern of the hero quest.

Before beginning to write this book, both of us had taught university courses on hero mythology—Jean in English literature courses and Wallace in religious studies courses. Having studied the psychology of C. G. Jung, we were familiar with the idea that the human psyche engages (when normal development occurs) in a lifelong process of growth and development. Furthermore, from our seminary studies we knew this was the same journey of growth and development which great Christians had sought to describe throughout history. When the hero pattern is understood in its complexity and not simply as a particular kind of melodrama, one can see that hero stories describe adventures frequently encountered on the journey of life.

Joseph Campbell's book *The Hero with a Thousand Faces* outlined this pattern and pointed out that hero stories were found in all cultures throughout human history.[1] The stories describe aspects of human experience that have been the experience of humanity at all times and in all places.

Jung's insights helped us to see that stories of the hero describe a growth in consciousness. Joseph Henderson and others have explored further the psychological significance of the motifs in hero stories.[2] The hero is someone who has learned something, gained a new perspective. Painful experiences can be a great teacher—if one lets them. They are often what one is presented with, both in life and hero stories. Hero mythology offers a grid or paradigm from which to view the journey of growth of the human spirit.

In our book *Symbols of Transformation in Dreams* we used the archetypes of the developmental process (identified in Jung's "path of individuation") as a backdrop against which to view those moments when dreams present one with symbols of transformation— the opportunity to expand one's horizon.[3] We referred briefly to the similarity of the path of individuation and the hero journey in that book, but since then we have come to appreciate in greater detail the complexity of the hero journey and its correspondence with the pattern of life's experiences. As one might expect, dreams, since they respond to the life being lived by the dreamer, resonate with those same motifs of the hero journey. In this book we describe and illustrate symbols of transformation in dreams that point to various stages or aspects of the hero journey.

In Chapter 1 we explore the role of story as an aid in discerning basic themes in one's behavior and psychological makeup. In Chapter 2 we describe Joseph Campbell's concept of the monomyth and the themes associated with the hero journey. In Chapter 3 we examine some of the ways human growth and development have been expressed. In Chapter 4 we consider the issues raised by feminist critiques of psychology and hero mythology in particular. Chapter 5 describes our approach to the interpretation of dreams and can be skipped by anyone who is familiar with C. G. Jung's understanding of the role of dreams and how they function in the psyche.

In Part II we take up the various motifs of the hero journey and illustrate those with dreams which we have been given permission to use anonymously (for which generous permission we again thank the dreamers). Each of five chapters in Part III contains a *series* of dreams of one individual and indicates how a development, sometimes involving the same symbol, can be observed in one individual's journey.

The Afterword summarizes the general relation of dreams, the hero monomyth, and the ordinary individual's personal and spiritual growth.

In the Appendix we suggest questions for reflection. These might be used as an aid in bringing one's own story or journey into perspective.

As was the case in our former work, much of this material has been honed in classrooms and seminars, and we have retained some of the informal mode of oral presentations. We have also used some illustrative material from our own lives, as well as those of others, and we have suggested several biblical stories which are illuminated by the hero pattern.

By these examples we seek to demonstrate that the essential meaning of the heroic quest continues to be useful when it is understood in its rich diversity and its essentially spiritual quality. The need for heroism in this sense is never outgrown, only deepened and expanded.

# Part I
# The Pattern of Life's Journey

*The hero's main feat is to overcome the monster of darkness: it is the long-hoped-for and expected triumph of consciousness over the unconscious.*

C. G. Jung

# Part 1

## The Pattern of Life's Journey

# ▶1
# Living a Story

Storytelling is one trait that all human beings have in common. Stories are told in the best of times and in the worst of times. Sometimes the stories are told with delight, sometimes with horror; sometimes they have profound import, sometimes little; sometimes they are interesting to the listener, sometimes tedious. Nevertheless, all cultures and peoples in all times have told stories. There are as many stories to tell as there are lives lived or imagined; storytelling is a well that never runs dry.

In some times and places, storytelling has been deemed frivolous, as if not worthy of attention by the serious student of human nature, but the twentieth century has returned respectability to the storyteller from a number of different fields. Studies in mythology and ethnology have demonstrated the crucial role stories play for any people. Feminist historians have focused on the necessity of adding women's stories to those which have been told and called "history." Religious studies have come to study the significance of the kinds of stories told about a faith without the exclusivity of the factual focus on historicity.

Several psychologists have enriched the study of human nature by their insights into the relation of story to human lives. Preeminently, C. G. Jung led the way. He realized that medical psychology, in order to be freed from what he called its "subjective and personalistic bias," had to study the entire wealth of the stories people have told and lived by; and these stories affect people in ways of which they are unconscious, as well as the conscious ways. Of course, the stories which form human behavior and attitudes in unconscious ways are much harder to become aware of. Jung's identification of the basic significance of these stories is one of his major contributions to psychology, and he devoted much of his long and fruitful life to their exploration.

In typically vivid prose Jung recounts how he felt when he realized that the stories which have been told and believed and lived by, or "myths," are absolutely necessary to creative human functioning:

> Hence the man who thinks he can live without myth, or outside it, is an exception. He is like one uprooted, having no true link either with the past, or with the ancestral life which continues within him, or yet with contemporary human society. He does not live in a house like other men, does not eat and drink like other men, but lives a life of his own, sunk in a subjective mania of his own devising, which he believes to be the newly discovered truth. This plaything of his reason never grips his vitals. It may occasionally lie heavy on his stomach, for that organ is apt to reject the products of reason as indigestible. The psyche is not of today; its ancestry goes back many millions of years. Individual consciousness is only the flower and the fruit of a season, sprung from the perennial rhizome beneath the earth; and it would find itself in better accord with the truth if it took the existence of the rhizome into its calculations.[1]

This realization struck home to Jung personally, as he was driven to ask himself what myth he himself was living. When he recognized that he had no idea, he challenged himself to find his own myth of meaning, thereafter considering his search for "his" myth to be the "task of tasks."[2] His work toward that end convinced him that the search for the myths one was living by was a most crucial search in the quest for consciousness and wholeness to which he believed all are called.

Rollo May also urges the importance of myth when he identifies three paths to knowledge of the unconscious: dreams, associations with images, and myth. In fact, he goes so far as to say, "Morality is the derivative of your myths."[3]

The first time we heard a lecturer speak on the subject of the importance of finding the myths and stories one lived by, the example given was a homely one. We were told of a woman who discovered one day that she was living the story of the "Little Red Hen." This common children's story tells of a little red hen who found some seed in the barnyard one day and called out to the other barnyard animals to help her plant it. They all made excuses for why they could not help her, and the little red hen said, "Well, I will then."

The story continues in the repetitive pattern of so many children's stories, as the little red hen asks for help at each stage—to water, weed, harvest, grind, and finally, to bake the bread. At each stage all the other animals declare themselves unable to help her, and she says, "Well, I will then."

Then, when it is time to eat the bread, all the animals volunteer to help the little red hen eat. In a version of the story our children had, the end of the story was "cleaned up," and the little red hen shared the bread with everyone. The original version of the story, however, has the little red hen reply, "No, I planted it, I watered it, I weeded it, I harvested it, I ground it, I baked it, and now I am going to eat it." The last paragraph of the book reads, "And she did."

The woman who "lived" the story of the little red hen discovered that her patterns of behavior typically matched those in the story. When she asked for help in any area (or even when there was just a task that needed to be done, say, in the family or office), she simply accepted the excuses given by others with a sweet little smile—and did the task by herself.

What the story suggests, of course, is that resentment builds up in the little red hen (even, we would add, if the little red hen is unconscious of the resentment), and someday the "worm will turn." Once this woman realized that she was continually acting out the story of the little red hen, she could identify her own typical behavior in each individual instance.

What does she do with the information? That decision is hers; she may make different decisions in different situations, of course. At one time she may decide that she would rather go ahead and *be* a little red hen, because the matter is not important enough to make an issue of it. Another time she may decide that enough is enough. Whatever she decides in each instance, she is making a more informed decision, with a much clearer awareness of the possible consequences of each choice.

There is another helpful aspect of thinking about one's behavior in terms of such a story: if one views oneself as acting like a little red hen, it is harder to be ponderous, overly serious, or too "holy" about oneself. In short, it is harder to become inflated or puffed up with one's own goodness and mistreatment by others. Life is placed in a lighter perspective; it is possible to have a healthy chuckle at oneself—and at the other "barnyard animals."

In psychological terms, the person who becomes aware of such patterns in her or himself is able to function in a more balanced and healthy way. The pattern is less likely to control him or her. Instead, the more conscious person can make more conscious choices. In spiritual terms, the more one knows about one's motives, the more one can become the person one is called by God to become. One becomes more freed from such destructive spirits as resentment and envy. With such an insight as the connection with the story of the little red hen, there is the additional positive factor of not taking oneself too seriously.

Two more examples, these from our own lives, may be helpful. After we heard this lecture on the little red hen, Jean began to search for her own myths or stories. This process can take a while, as does any attempt to make something conscious which has been unconscious. The first storybook character she identified in her behavior patterns was the little toy clown from a children's book called *The Little Engine That Could*.

In that story the engine breaks down on a train carrying dolls and toys to the children on the other side of the mountain. All the dolls and toys begin to cry because the children on the other side of the mountain won't have any dolls and toys to play with, but the little toy clown jumps up and calls for everyone to cheer up—theirs isn't the only engine in the world and surely someone else will help them. Then follow several scenes in which the little toy clown flags down other engines and presents the problem to them, only to be knocked rudely aside. Each time the dolls and toys begin to cry, and each time the little toy clown repeats his theology of hope, backed up with the action of flagging down more engines.

Finally a very little engine offers to help them and struggles up the mountain with the now-famous line "I think I can. I think I can." After the engine successfully negotiates the top, the line changes to the triumphant "I thought I could, I thought I could."

That story was balanced later by the realization of another story that Jean lived by—Chicken Little. A nut falls on Chicken Little one day, and she immediately decides, "The sky is falling!" She runs to find the wise owl to give her advice. On the way, she runs into a number of other barnyard birds, who ask her (sensibly) how she knows the sky is falling. She always replies (not quite truthfully), "I saw it with my eyes. I heard it with my ears. Some of it fell on my tail."

All the other birds join her until the whole crowd reaches the owl, who says (skeptically requiring more than hearsay proof), "Let me see the sky that fell on you. Then I will tell you what to do." Chicken Little leads them back to the place where she was when the panic hit. After looking around, they find the nut, at which the owl laughs and says, "You want me to tell you what to do. Laugh, Chicken Little, and we will too."

Chicken Little, probably an extravert intuitive personality type like Jean, panics and *thinks* she has perceived the end of the world with her sensate functions of seeing and hearing. In fact, of course, her very panic prevents her from using these less well-developed functions until she gets some help from her friend the owl, this folk tale's wisdom figure.

The patterns of these two stories helped Jean identify similar patterns in her own behavior. They also showed her a danger in overidentifying with one part of herself—the little toy clown part. In other words, the two stories seem to be a pair psychologically. If one blindly adheres to the little toy clown optimism, no matter how great a gift it is, without staying aware of the world of external reality, one can make foolish mistakes by being overwhelmed by external reality.

Jung noted that when we push something down into the unconscious, it does not simply go away. Rather, it stays down there, gathering energy and getting ready to burst out unexpectedly. He called this process by its classical name, *enantiodromia*—the regulative function of the opposites whereby a consciously held view which becomes too extreme has a tendency to turn into its opposite. Consciousness needs to operate in full awareness of the grim possibilities in the unconscious.

These two stories—the little toy clown and Chicken Little—together bring a sense of perspective. Jean found it hard to take herself quite so seriously in the midst of some daily panic; who can feel tragic when she sees herself behaving like Chicken Little? She could also spot her tendency to cling frantically on occasion to the little toy clown pattern. All in all, the stories have been a big help through the years.

It might be noted that a part of their helpfulness lies in the essentially positive nature of the two characters. They are nice characters who need to watch out not to get too extreme. Together they make up a personality type which, exercised pathologically, would be called manic-depressive. We suggest that the identification of the stories one lives by carries with it the positive healing potential lacking in many descriptions of pathology and thus becomes a powerful therapeutic growth tool.

Even the realization of the negative portions of our inner storybook characters is an aid to consciousness. No matter how bad the news is of one's inner shadow possibilities, it is better to know it than not to know it. It is in the knowing that the ability to overcome lies. One who will not face the shadow within will not grow toward greater maturity. Even here, the realization that the shadow tendencies are part of a story—clearly demonstrating that other people have shared such tendencies before us—has healing potential.

These stories are much smaller examples than the cultural myths of a whole people or a religious tradition, yet Jung was right in saying that even such simple stories are important psychologically. If they are told and remembered, it is probably because they capture some truth about human functioning which speaks to people about themselves. It is from these truths that stories are psychologically significant, whether they are "true" stories or not.

Individuals can search for their own lived stories not only by watching their behavior patterns, but also by reflecting on stories which captured their imagination very early in life. People frequently find that stories they loved or hated as children reveal significant information about their inner patterns. Their own hopes, joys, fears, and pains were evidently projected onto stories which thus carried strong emotional content for them.

One's earliest memory can also be a clue to the pattern of one's life story. Wallace's earliest memory, for example, is of running into the yard and thinking, "I am three years old." The tone of the thought was reflective; the reflection concerned his childish wonder at the significance of being three. In later years he could see this concern with *significance* and reflection on it as a typical pattern for an introverted thinking type such as he.

The stories he remembers reading avidly as a boy were the adventures of Richard Halliburton, who swam the Hellespont, traveled to Timbuktu and the Sahara Desert, waded in the reflecting pool of the Taj Mahal, and climbed the Matterhorn. He can remember daydreaming of all those places, and, in fact, his main elementary school reading was the *National Geographic,* over which he pored, lying on the living room floor. A little later, his main doodling was drawing maps of imaginary countries.

This longing of his heart seems more related psychologically to his goals than to his behavior patterns—to what he longed to do, rather than how he did it. We have speculated that Jean's stories, reflecting how she functioned, may be more related to feeling function than Wallace's stories, which reflect a more goal-oriented thinking function.

In actual fact, Wallace began traveling at seventeen and has seldom stopped for very long since then. In the university, he was challenged to the exploration of the social realm from a spiritual viewpoint—a spirit that taught peace in time of war and worked for integration in a segregated university. After midlife, this exploration also focused on the exploration of the inner world. Today, he would understand all these explorations as resonating with his early adventure story and geographic reading.

Journaling has long been an excellent way to get in touch with the story one is living, not only in its general form or pattern, but in its individuality. People have used journals and autobiographical writings for centuries to apprehend and describe their journeys of self-discovery. Ira Progoff's system of Intensive Journal Workshops, published in his books from Dialogue House, has proved helpful to thousands.[4] This mode of journaling is designed to incorporate both conscious and unconscious parts of the journaler into a process in which conscious and unconscious aid each other and interact.

Progoff designed his Intensive Journal after a detailed study of the processes of creative people. From this he determined that the primary component of creativity is the dialogue between consciousness and unconsciousness, the process Jung called "active imagination." Such journaling gets one in touch with the movement and rhythm of one's life story. A fascinating apsect of Progoff's discoveries is that even nearly illiterate people can benefit from such journaling, as if the journaling itself teaches them that they, too, have a story which matters in the world.

In another sense, all people have a number of stories they live by, which come together in their life stories. Some of these stories are taught them by their families. The stories that are told in families form a part of who we are regardless of whether we remain close to the family or rebel against it. We do not mean to suggest that one must inevitably live under some limitation handed down from generation to generation with no possibility of escape. We do assert that family stories are a part of the equation of life with which everyone must come to terms.

Like other influential stories, family stories may be either limiting or life enhancing. A family pattern of achievement or public service, for example, may inspire a family member to emulate the family tradition. On the other hand, some family traditions may be experienced as life destroying. The typical example is of the father who demands that his son follow his chosen field of work or study, despite the son's different interests and abilities. In many traditional cultures such family determinism was an accepted part of life; born of a king, one was a king; born of a blacksmith, one was a blacksmith.

The lack of any family stories at all is also very sad. Life and literature abound with tales of people abandoned or left as sole survivors with no remaining family. Such folk must work hard to reconstitute an understanding of who they are without the containing presence of family stories. Sensitive work is being done in this century with children, orphaned victims of war, who are adopted into other families, races, and cultures; they are being brought up in their adoptive homes with intentional teaching about the homes from which they came as children.

Many people who enter analysis find that they are led to reflect back on the family stories which formed their backdrop as a way of coming to understand their own lives. This can be another helpful way to explore one's life story. For example, Wallace, in reflecting on his family heritage, realized that his ancestors had been moving to new lands for centuries. One of his grandfathers, for instance, in trying to decide where to settle, traveled aross the country from the

East Coast to Seattle at a time when travel was not easy. Some of Wallace's exploring tendencies may be in his genes.

His other grandfather was a man whose life was changed by a religious experience. This is a part of the background of his own inner explorations. Again, we are not suggesting that one is determined by family history, but only that family stories are another way to understand the stories one lives by.

Another level of stories which affects people is that of the stories of the larger groups of which these people are a part. Religious communities tell their stories, and this becomes a major part of the individual members' self-understanding. The Christian Church, for example, has been called "the people who remember Jesus." As James Fowler, the premier theorist of how faith develops, puts it, Christians are "a story-born people." He says the content of faith *is* the stories, including the rituals in which the stories are "encoded."[5] Judaism, Buddhism, Hinduism, Islam, and all the other religions tell their stories of their relation to God or the gods, of their founders, their saints and heroes—in short, of the charism of their beginnings. Fowler says individuals and religious traditions seek interesting ways to tell their stories and how to get the stories moving again when they are stuck.

Tribes and races tell their stories, and these are part of the identity of those who descend from them. The book and the television series *Roots* influenced many to look again toward their own roots as a part of claiming their racial and family history. The modern state of Israel claims its history as a kind of destiny connected with the land. Native American Indians and Australian aborigines, to name only two groups, are also asserting their claims to their land and their heritage.

In the book *Australia's Kakadu Man* an anthropologist records the words of an old aboriginal man, Big Bill Neidjie. Bill, as his tribe's storyteller, has a duty to pass on the wisdom accumulated from the experience of *two thousand or more generations*—over fifty thousand years! From his hope that his own children and others would "hang onto" this knowledge, he made the deliberate decision to entrust the stories to someone who would write them. He ends his story with these words:

>   You got children . . .
>   grandson.

> Might be your grandson will get this story . . .
> keep going . . .
> hang on like I done.[6]

This is the recognition that the survival of the story is an element of the survival of meaning. The aborigines need to remember their stories in order to be.

Laurens van der Post, speaking about the African companions with whom he grew up, says, "These people lived without ever losing their central conviction that a story truly told is a kind of religious experience without which life itself is diminished in colour and meaning."[7]

In the last half of this century, technologically advanced nations are struggling with how to understand their own stories. The United States and Australia, celebrating the bicentennial of their "countries," have had to face the stories of the people who were there before European settlement. The countries of Europe wrestle with how a holocaust can still grasp them despite their centuries of civilization and education.

Yet much of this struggle to understand comes in rational, logical examinations of cause and effect. This is useful, of course, but Jung and others suggest that the living symbols of stories, simple tale or cosmic myth, operate within us at a much deeper level than the rational consciousness. They have the power to move, to challenge, to change people and cultures. Grasping our stories—or better, being grasped by them—is central to the pilgrimage of the human spirit.

# ▶2

# The Monomyth

Jung wrote that the inner voice is the voice of a fuller life and a wider, more comprehensive consciousness. "That is why," he said, "in mythology, the birth of the hero or the symbolic rebirth coincides with sunrise, for the growth of personality is synonymous with an increase of self-consciousness." And, he continued, "The problems of the inner voice are full of pitfalls and hidden snares. Treacherous, slippery ground, as dangerous and pathless as life itself once one lets go of the railings. But he who cannot lose his life, neither shall he save it. The hero's birth and the heroic life are always threatened."[1]

Joseph Campbell, in *The Hero with a Thousand Faces,* analyzed the pattern of hero myths and stories from all ages and places. He called this pattern the *monomyth,* the one great myth that humans have told for centuries. It is found everywhere because it is a story of human life. In the diagram on page 15 we have modified and adapted Campbell's diagram of the monomyth. Basically, there are three parts: departure, initiation, and return.

### Departure

There is a moving away from the home place, in whatever way that is described. The hero departs from the way things have been. There may have been a dissatisfaction with the status quo or boredom with the way things were. The question of departure from the home place often entails what Campbell called the "call to adventure." This may involve a new look at the situation at home. The signs of the vocation of the hero may be indicated in the story: a special birth, an astrological prediction, or a cosmic event. There may be a refusal of the call to adventure; it seems too scary or unpredictable. The obstacles to departure may seem insurmountable.

## Initiation

The threshold of adventure has to be crossed; there is a separation. It may involve a descent into the netherworld, a cave, a pit, hell, or a journey through a wilderness. This stage is sometimes decribed as the "road of trials," for there are tests and tasks that may have to be performed, and the hero is tempted to turn aside at every step. There are various encounters on the journey—perhaps supernatural aid: helpful or friendly animals (instincts and other parts of the psyche come to the aid of the ego undertaking the journey of development). There may be an encounter with a member of the opposite sex, a tempter or temptress, who can and would divert one from the journey, or so it seems at first. Then, with the accomplishment of the task—the slaying of the dragon, or the finding of the treasure, or the receiving of the blessing or gift—the hero has new power. Something has been accomplished and the hero is a new person.

## Return

Next comes the question of return, of taking the treasure home. The return may be refused. The new country is too delightful, why bother with others? There is a return threshold to be crossed, with all its dangers. If the hero follows through, the return is made and the hero brings home the treasure to share with the people at home. In a sense, the hero is now a "master of two worlds." The problems of the situation at home may be solved; the hero may found a new society or the boon brought home may simply provide a new freedom to live. The story may describe a royal wedding, which symbolizes the union of two worlds. For the hero, the return involves a reintegration into society.

In fairy tales the hero is often the rejected child—perhaps a stepchild—who, for one reason or another, has to leave the home place. In many stories it is the youngest child who succeeds where older siblings failed, suggesting perhaps that the hero journey requires

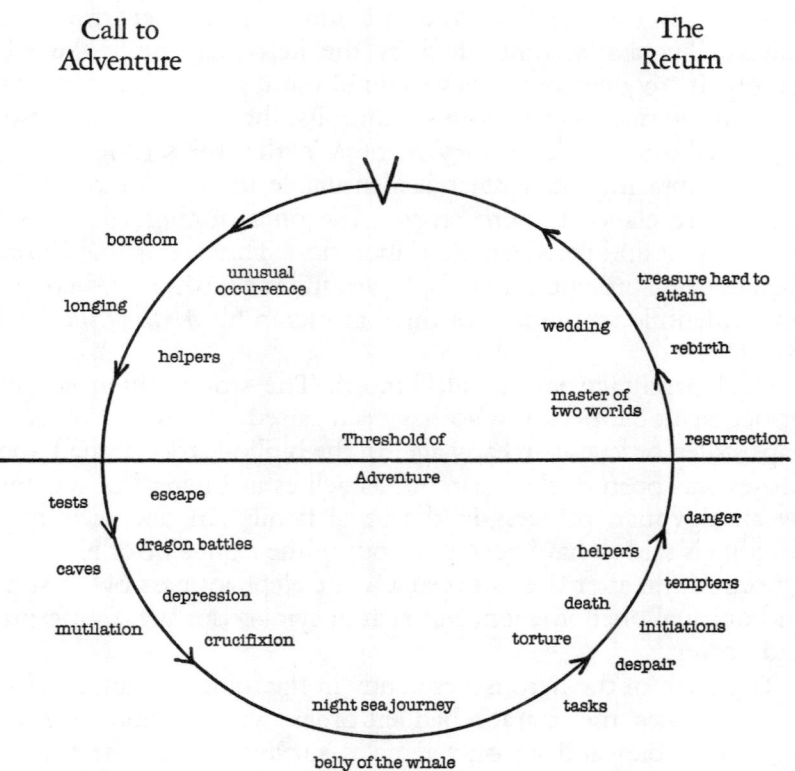

innocence or a less rigid view of the world. The treasure won may benefit only the family or the individual. In the hero myths of a culture the task accomplished by the hero may serve the whole nation. It frequently involves some physical accomplishment; however, in the stories of religious traditions, the victory won is usually portrayed as an ethical achievement. Whether the setting is local or world embracing, the pattern is identifiable and varies little.

In more elaborate hero stories, the ones dealing with a whole people, you find considerable elaboration. There are some common themes often present, for example, around the birth of the hero. Otto Rank identified a number of these motifs in his *Myth of the Birth of the Hero*.[2]

Dual parentage is one such motif. The stories often involve a prince or noble person who has been raised by lowly parents, perhaps stolen or lost at an early age. In the biblical story of the Exodus, Moses was born to slave parents, Israelites in Egypt, but was raised by an Egyptian princess in the royal family. In one account, the Buddha is said to have been born out of the right side of his mother, Queen Maya, after she had seen a white elephant pass by—a strange and unusual phenomenon, but rich in symbolism suggesting purity and power.

The birth of the hero is frequently in the midst of dangers. In the case of Moses, the pharaoh had left orders with the midwives to kill all male babies and let only females survive because he feared an uprising of his Hebrew slaves. For the Buddha, born of a king of a city-state in northern India, the "danger" came from the father. Court astrologers had predicted at his birth that the son would become either a great ruler or a holy man in the Indian religious tradition. The father feared the latter and according to traditional stories did all he could to prevent his young son from being bothered by questions that religious philosophies sought to answer.

In hero stories the hero must fight with dragons—dragons from within and dragons from without (not always in the same story). The inner dragon is the unconscious pull to stay still, not to "wake up," to maintain a purely instinctual response to life rather than to live a life of reflection and understanding. On the other hand, the outer dragon is society's demand for conformity or, more insidiously, society's suggestion that the statistical average of "what everyone is doing" is the behavioral norm. Yet doing battle with both dragons is necessary to release the creative energy within oneself and in the world. Responding to one's own vocation or calling is not as easy as it would appear. Coming to consciousness is a heroic task.

This battle with the dragons is an old one in spiritual growth. Flannery O'Connor mentions in one of her letters a passage from the early church, where Cyril of Jerusalem instructs catechumens with this warning: "The dragon is at the side of the road watching those who pass. Take care lest he devour you: You are going to the Father of souls, but it is necessary to pass by the dragon."[3]

An anomalous attitude toward the word *hero* exists today. On the one hand, some treat it as an image of courage and achievement in the face of difficult odds—an honorable word of recognition and admiration. This is probably the older meaning. On the other hand, *hero* is sometimes used pejoratively, as an epithet of derision, describing a kind of mindless self-centeredness and selfishness. Or *hero* is sometimes used derisively to refer to someone who always acts right and looks good—the cowboy in the white hat from Saturday movie matinees, one who has no shadow side. In this book we use the word in its older mode, in an attempt to illustrate its value by connecting the hero journey to the development of human personality and character. In other words, in using the term *hero* we do not mean an inflated ego trip, but rather we see the task of proper ego development as reflecting the motifs of the classic hero journey.

Jung makes a similar distinction, identifying "absolute" heroes who operate in "an infantile defiance to a fate greater than they, or else a pomposity meant to cover up some touchy inferiority." He contrasts this with "humdrum" and "banal" everyday demands, of which he says, "For us to fulfill these demands (as we must) humbly and without courting applause through heroic gestures, a heroism is needed that cannot be seen from the outside. It does not glitter, is not belauded, and it always seeks concealment in everyday attire. These are the demands which, if not fulfilled, are the cause of neurosis."[4]

Creation myths can be found in most, if not all, of the world's cultures. Understood psychologically, they describe in pictorial language the experience of either the beginning of consciousness or the coming to consciousness of a fragment of experience. Hero myths can be said to be creation myths in microcosm, for they are stories about the task of *creation* within the individual, as, for example, becoming aware of something or learning something. The individual may serve the whole society—often the case for important culture heroes—but the task is one heroes accomplish within themselves. They may have help, but it is ultimately an inward integration that must take place. If the hero is able to follow through, then there is a new release of creative energy available. This may be used for personal enhancement, but if the hero is true to the whole task in the basic pattern of the hero story, it is used for others. In the completed hero story, the hero brings back the treasure for the tribe, the community, or the world.

On the journey the hero becomes a different person. It is ultimately a story of transformation, of growth. Sometimes the growth is in strength of a physical sort, but usually it is a growth in "wisdom." The hero returns home a wiser person, a more developed, a more humane person. This is what the hero has to share with the tribe or the culture. To achieve this, the hero has to undergo trials and hardships and do battle with all sorts of things. There may be some pain in parting, a difficulty about leaving the home territory. The "foreign" is usually a bit frightening. The hero may be tempted to stay in the distant land rather than undertake the difficult journey back home, with the possibility of more dangers and trials.

The hero must usually "abandon all" and yet very likely also have the experience of being abandoned. It is a lonely journey, with friends and helpers along the way sometimes, but it is still something the hero undertakes alone. Like Jonah in the biblical story the hero must make the "night sea journey" in the belly of the whale, or like Jesus descend into hell, or like Joseph be lowered into the pit and sold into slavery by his brothers, or like Moses travel the wilderness—the symbolical world of the "other." The hero's preparation for achieving the heights is to plumb the depths. The search for wisdom, for wholeness, for integration, has been reflected in the stories of every culture, for it is the story of the experience of human development. There is a pattern for spiritual growth and development for humans—just as physically children grow into adults.

Of course, life has unfolded according to its natural course of development throughout human history. The "developmental tasks" in human life have not come into being with modern psychology. Psychologists have merely described what they see happening in the course of human development and what they see as the goal of human development. But long before, people all around the world were telling stories about their experience of life—of what it meant to be human. Some of the stories dealt with only parts of life's experience. Others dealt with bigger aspects, and some tended to give an overview of the whole development.

The hero story or myth, in its myriad forms, gives expression to the basic tasks of human development. The tasks are many and the hero journey may have to be experienced over and over—throughout life—but at different levels of understanding. As Jungian analyst and psychiatrist James Hall has said, "In the process of individuation there is no single creative or heroic act, but rather a succession of transformations over a lifetime, each straining and testing the ego anew—a series of what Neumann referred to as calvaries."[5]

Some hero stories deal with tasks of the first half of life. They may be concerned with building an identity, establishing oneself as somebody in the world. That task involves a "going out"—explorations, perhaps an acquiring of something or doing some task and making it one's own. It becomes a part of one's identity. The new experiences of young people become a part of who they are. These tasks of the first half of life have a heroic quality about them.

Then, too, in what Jung called "the second half of life," there are other tasks which should culminate in the finding of some meaning in the whole business of life. This entails also a "going out" from the ego position one has established and encountering an "other"—a larger meaning than just oneself. One of the motifs here is *sacrifice*, a motif found in so many of the world's religions. Understood psychologically, it is a sacrifice of the ego: the ego gives up something of itself in order to be in relationship with a larger meaning. The language of the religious traditions varies. In Islam it is submission to Allah. In Judaism and Christianity it is more often described as entering a relationship with God. However the symbol system describes the process, it involves a free offering of oneself, a giving up—at least in part—of the ego position. The peculiar thing about this is that in giving up something of yourself you find you are more truly yourself than ever before. This is the paradox of the Christian journey and of other religious traditions. It is the "wisdom" acquired in all hero journeys concerned with the developmental tasks of the second half of life.

How, then, can the monomyth pattern be helpful to understand human growth? We follow Campbell in suggesting that the mythic patterns of stories are illuminating for personal self-understanding.[6] The stages of the hero myth are "the constituent elements in the personal development of every individual."[7] The hero journey is one way of describing the task of becoming truly human. It is also one of the three archetypal aspects of healing which, Donald Sandner says, "have served the main healing function for the entire human race for a period of time that can only be measured in millenia [sic]." The hero journey is thus one image of the themes of death and rebirth, breakdown and renewal, and it functions in the individual outside of conscious intention.[8]

This movement toward wholeness is depicted by various motifs of marriage, reconciliation, and community celebration. In literature such "fairy tale endings" are frequently deprecated as unrealistic, "as if dialectical division were more literalily legitimate than resolution," as one critic writes. She adds, however, the incisive comment that hero stories are in fact modern fairy tales, "and fairy tales do end in the happily-ever-after feeling produced when psyches are made whole."[9] Thus we would also argue that when the hero journey is psychologically understood in its entirety, such happy endings are appropriate.

Telling one's own stories or getting in touch with the stories which help identify one's behavior is helpful in and of itself. Even more (suggested but not developed by Campbell), dreams can be interpreted in the light of the monomyth pattern. The motifs and images of the dream can be identified as belonging to a given place on the hero's circle. If a dream image suggests that the dreamer is receiving a call to adventure, for example, the current life situation is illuminated by that awareness.

The examples in this book will attempt to demonstrate that the motifs common to hero journeys—or the "keys," as Campbell calls them—can help to interpret similar motifs or images in dreams. This in turn helps place the life situation in a helpful perspective; each person can understand his or her dreams against the monomyth grid and thus understand what is going on with a new objectivity. As consciousness always does, this enables more informed and conscious choices to be made.

## ▶3

# The Human Journey

All cultures have responded in some way to the facts of human growth and the development of the human spirit. Stories that resonate with the experiences of life have been told over and over; and so in the world's fairy tales, mythologies, and religious stories one finds represented the facts of human experience. As we have suggested, this is particularly true in the hero stories found in all cultures. Another way of expressing this human journey is through religious and community rites.

Early in this century Arnold van Gennep described in *The Rites of Passage* three customary stages of such rites: separation from one social status, a transition stage, and finally, incorporation into another social status.[1] These three stages also describe most initiation rituals, and they constitute the basic pattern of the hero journey—Joseph Campbell's monomyth.

Mircea Eliade identified the essential purpose of initiation: to produce a decisive alteration in the status of the initiate, both religiously and socially. "In philosophical terms," he says, "initiation is equivalent to a basic change in existential condition; the novice emerges from the ordeal endowed with a totally different being from that which he possessed before his initiation; he has become *another*." Furthermore, Eliade concludes, "the same initiatory patterns are found in the dreams and in the imaginative life both of modern men and of the primitive."[2]

Social anthropologist Victor Turner has given special attention to the middle stage, referring to it as one of "liminality," where one is confronted with the ambiguity associated with being between stages, being "no longer" one thing and "not yet" another. A recent anthology, *Betwixt and Between: Patterns of Masculine and Feminine Initiation,* explores in a number of essays both the personal meaning for the individual and the social significance of the experience of liminality and the role of initiation rituals. In her introduction to the collection of essays, Louise Carus Mahdi says, "Where have all the elders gone? We cannot provide initiations at puberty—or earlier or later—unless we have elders with some knowledge of these processes and what aspects of initiation could be applicable today."[3] Jungian analyst Joseph Henderson could perhaps be said to be one such elder. In his *Thresholds of Initiation* he has described "the archetype of initiation" and illustrated its variety of manifestations in the literary imagination and in the dreams of contemporary people. He writes, "Since modern man cannot return to his origins in any collective sense, he apparently is tempted and even forced to return to them in an individual way at certain times in his personal development."[4]

Victor and Edith Turner have identified the initiatory quality found in pilgrimages in *Image and Pilgrimage in Christian Culture: Anthropological Perspectives*. They write, "A pilgrim is one who divests himself of the mundane concomitants of religion—which become entangled with its practice in the local situation—to confront, in a special 'far' milieu, the basic elements and structures of his faith in their unshielded, virgin radiance."[5] The same three stages are involved. There is a departure, the encounters of the "pilgrimage" along the way, and a return. Even though the pilgrimage does entail a return to the home place, the pilgrim is a changed person and has a different contribution to make to the community. Pilgrimage and initiatory rites in general indicate the basic pattern of spiritual growth and psychological development.

Henderson distinguishes the hero myth from an initiation rite. He uses "hero myth" to refer to the struggles of breaking out of the confines of the unconscious, that is, from childhood, and the struggle that breaking away involves. The initiation rite focuses on a symbolic death and rebirth. The task may well involve, he says, submission to a power greater than oneself.[6] As we suggested earlier, *sacrifice* is often a prominent motif in hero stories.

We prefer to use "hero journey" to refer to the whole spectrum of life, as the threefold pattern of the hero journey identified by Joseph

Campbell seems to us to include both the initiation and the consciousness motifs. The paradigm of the hero journey provides a helpful model for organizing the experiences of life. When initiation rites are not available, as they seldom are in contemporary society, dreams may provide the necessary symbols.

There is an identity of fundamental human conflicts which is independent of time and place. Thus, when myths speak to you, they do so in the present tense. Typically the story tells how things were in the past, how something came into being, or how things were in the beginning, but when you find yourself drawn to any particular myth—when you find a story worth retelling—the reality of your present experience is in some measure being portrayed. Myths tell it like it is. Primitives did not *invent* myths, Jung says, they *experienced* them.[7] Joseph Campbell says, "Mythology is psychology misread as biography, history and cosmology!"[8] If he is correct that myths are psychology, as we think he is, then understood psychologically, myths can help one to discern the patterns and motifs in one's own life story. Long ago Aristotle observed that tragedy was cathartic for spectators, for (when well done) spectators live out the tragedy within themselves; and, similarly, one's emotional response to a myth suggests a personal inner significance.

Spiritual growth, like all growth, requires a change of attitude—a leaving behind of the old and an opening up of the possibility of the new. It feels like a journey. In a sense, all learning requires this. Youngsters in elementary school are excited about going to the next grade, but also sometimes awed by whether they can do what is required, for example, in "high" school.

Committing oneself to another partner for life is scary business. Some people have difficulty summoning the courage to take the step. Marriage is serious. One gives up something of one's independence. Taking on the nurture and care for a new life (having a baby) is another major transition in life, and it inevitably necessitates a change in the parent—usually (but not always) for the better. Having a child breaks one out of the shell of one's self, just as marriage does.

The great transition moments in life, or "rites of passage," are expressed in ritual. The purpose and actual effect of these rituals is to conduct people across those difficult thresholds of transformation that demand a change in the patterns not only of conscious but also of unconscious life. Primitive societies responded to this, largely on an unconscious level, but nevertheless effectively and always symbolically—for symbols are the carriers of ultimate meaning.

Primitive rites of passage—particularly those around puberty, marking the transition from childhood to adulthood—were generally characterized by severe exercises of severance or separation whereby the mind was radically cut away from the attitudes, attachments, and life patterns of the stage being left behind. There was often (for this particular rite of passage) a period of isolation and then induction and training in the proper attitudes and feelings for the person's new life situation. The initiates might be taken to a cave or a hut deep in the forest and there subjected to various tests and trials, such as traditional lacerations or circumcision; they might also be required to learn the sacred rituals and myths appropriate to their new status as adults. The rites usually included some orientation into what it means to be an adult woman or an adult man.

Religious traditions, of course, have also generally had rites to mark these occasions: circumcision, baptism, naming, bar mitzvah, confirmation, marriage ceremonies, and burials. These rites, as well as the structures of a great variety of cultural and social rites, have the same basic pattern van Gennep identified. This can be seen in rites as varied as becoming a naturalized citizen and ritual toasts.[9]

In the case of Christianity, the ceremony celebrating the movement from childhood to adulthood has generally been relegated to a date too early to be realistic or even deemphasized or ignored. In the case of Judaism, the often elaborate celebration after the religious ceremony at least makes it memorable. In the secular world, as experienced in the United States, about all there is to mark this transition is the obtaining of a driver's license or a school graduation exercise.

In the more catholic traditions of Christianity there is a rite which anthropologists would not think of as a "rite of passage," but which marks a transition from one attitude to another: confession or the rite of reconciliation. It marks an occasion for spiritual growth. In analysis, pastoral counseling, or work with a spiritual director, there are seldom rites, but there are occasions for joy when the counselee has withdrawn a projection or recognized a shadow involvement in a situation.

The Sufi tradition teaches that all values, beliefs, and destructive actions of the past can be transformed through dreams for one who is seriously on the inner journey: "One second of dream suffering is like three years of real suffering in life. When you are on the path you are speeded up, and you pay for it in your dreams." The spiritual teachings of the Hasidic tradition in Judaism encourage a ritual dance after counseling sessions with the rebbe, so that the new wholeness may be carried to deeper levels in the music and movement.[10]

All these rites of passage are, in a sense, *initiation rituals* that seek to call attention to what has been left behind, and what lies ahead. It has always been the prime function of mythology and rituals to supply the symbols that carry the human spirit forward, in counteraction to those ever-present temptations to stay still and not "rock the boat."

The temptation is to stay in a safe place. Jungian analyst Luigi Zoja says that in the modern world, where so much is programed and "safe" in life, the lack of initiation rituals has driven many to a negative kind of "initiation" in various addictions. With society failing to provide initiations, the task of coming up with demanding initiatory rites has fallen to institutions which help people get rid of addictions.[11] Edith Sullwold makes a similar point about teenage suicides, which have increased so dramatically in recent years. She says such suicides may occur "because of an intense desire for change—a hopelessness in life as it is"—and points to the need for more conscious rites of passage.[12]

The psyche is programed for growth just as the body is programed for growth. Contemporary culture has often been unaware of this. Frequently "religions" have been thought to be outmoded—to belong to the "childhood of the race." But interestingly, it is the rite-of-passage ceremonies of religious traditions that are often still sought. People return to a religious tradition for baptisms, weddings, and funerals. Jung called the world's great religions the world's great psychotherapeutic symbol systems precisely because religions provide symbols by which the individual psyche can be carried forward in its growth and development. As Jung once said, "The very fact that you live the symbolic life has an extraordinarily civilizing influence."[13]

On the American frontier, as people moved west by foot, wagon, and horseback, Protestants tended to do away with many rituals in their religious services; however, secret societies flourished, with elaborate initiation rituals (some entailing a symbolic death and resurrection or "raising up"). Many initiation rituals exist today in an atrophied state, but they usually entail in their more elaborate forms the same pattern as the hero stories. They dramatize the movement from one position or status to another.

A major use of symbolism today is by the advertising industry. The use of symbols in advertising functions largely on the unconscious level. One often does not realize why one buys one shampoo instead of another. The advertising industry proves the power of symbols to function on an unconscious level. With the loss of appreciation of symbolic language to a large extent, contemporary culture has deprived itself of the clues and the road map for the development and growth of the spirit. Our purpose in exploring the motifs of the hero journey is to relearn or increase our vocabulary in the language of symbolism.

The task of spiritual growth of an individual is related to the culture, the spiritual milieu, in which the individual is enmeshed. Developmental theory points out that the place where a person is seems ultimate; one is *embedded* in the world view of the present. Then, if the complexity of life no longer can be explained by the present world view, the person finds a new need to make sense or find meaning out of the new reality with which he or she is faced. Robert Kegan suggests that this meaning-making process is how people grow, as they break through to another level of meaning, which is more complex and thus more able to deal with present reality. He says the new meaning is qualitatively different from the old meaning, and the process of moving from one to another consistently follows the pattern of "defending, surrendering, and reconstructing a center."[14] He describes the effect of this in two ways: one "is moved to make meaning or to resolve discrepancy; but this would not be different than to say [one] is moved to preserve and enhance [one's] integrity." One separates oneself from the old world view sufficiently to see that it *is* a world view and thus one is no longer embedded in it. This sounds very much like the journey on which the hero travels.

The challenge to grow is different for each individual even within the same culture. No one life is the same as another. Jungian psychology suggests that there is a developmental tendency toward the unique. In fact, in the definition of "hero" which we are suggesting, individuality in all its complexity is precisely the psychological significance of the hero myth.

With culture heroes this individuality is sometimes threatened; the culture may tell only part of the hero's story—the part which confirms its point of view. These are some of the times when "hero" seems to be someone too good to be true. For example, Joan of Arc, like many famous culture heroes, has been interpreted for several centuries by different groups, all of which tend to omit some of her story to make her fit their ideal. Marina Warner has traced this history of interpretation of Joan, commenting that in the end Joan herself stands beyond these distortions:

> She stands for an integrity that is not subject to decay, that was saved from spoiling by a glorious end, and so she can act as the talisman of people or of nations who feel themselves endangered. She has been set up as a stable monolith in a unstable world, and yet all the different uses to which she has been put prove only the vanity of our widespread refusal to accept that it is impossible to trap the idea of virtue within boundaries that will not alter.[15]

The hero journey about which we are writing is the inner journey of an individual—the response to vocation or "calling." There are two aspects to vocation. First, there is the "calling" experienced through the unconscious, as if from "outside," a feeling that one is required to do this or that or perhaps experienced only as a deep longing without quite knowing why or what for. Second, there is the response the individual makes to the calling. Considerable effort may be required; courage is called for in engaging the new and unknown.

In the theistic religious traditions of the West, the hero is regarded as "chosen" by God or the gods to accomplish the task. In the Gnostic and humanistic "counterculture" of the West, accomplishment is viewed as the result of the hard work of an individual. Both perspectives can be seen as true if, first, one acknowledges the role of the creative unconscious, which issues a "call to adventure" and provides some "helpful animals" along the way; and second, one recognizes that courage is required to answer the call as well as hard work to "win the treasure." Emphasis on the first produces a sense of being "chosen," with aid coming from "outside." Emphasis on the second calls attention to the personal bravery and difficulties encountered in the achievement. In the traditional hero stories of cultures around the world both aspects of the journey tend to be set forth.

The task of the hero journey might also be described as discovering how to live within a symbol system and know, at the same time, that it is a symbol system. The great religious thinkers of India have been able to do this. They describe it symbolically, but the popular devotion of the mass of people still takes the symbol "concretely," as Tillich might say. Many people in the West, in Christianity and Judaism, have also found their way through this obstacle. For many, however, it is an obstacle, for the Western religious traditions start with a focus on the concrete. The first story in the Scriptures is one describing the creation of the material world and how God was pleased with the creation—finding it "good."

Some years ago, twentieth-century New Testament scholar John Knox formulated the question this way: how can one have myths (as one must to be religious) and at the same time know that they are myths (as one must if one is modern)?[16] More recently, theologians have wrestled with the question and have begun writing about "theology and story" or "theology as story." Paul Ricoeur has described this journey of increasing consciousness and appreciation of a symbol as a symbol (and not merely a sign) as a movement in three stages: first, a naive relation to the symbol (as with much popular devotion); second, dismissing the symbol as a "nothing but" (as with the concretistic reduction of some demythologizers); and third, recovering what he called a "second naivete."[17] Joseph Campbell has suggested that since the function of mythology is to carry the human spirit forward, perhaps its loss in the modern world is the cause of "modern neuroticism."[18]

The pilgrimage of the human spirit entails a development of consciousness, the gaining of a wider perspective. It is a movement toward wisdom. Contrary to popular understanding and a nonsymbolical reading of mythology, heroes are actually made—not born. They develop through life experience. Heroes, one could way, are those who have had their consciousness raised.

# ▶4

# Gender and Journey

Can women be heroes? We answer a resounding yes to that frequently asked question. Heroes may be either male or female. Partly, of course, this depends on the way one uses *hero*. We use the word *hero* to include both men and woman, in part because the usual feminine form *heroine* tends to connote a person who is rescued, a passive recipient of help, not a helper or a mover and shaker. We consequently prefer to use *hero* in a gender-free way. Our only use of *heroine* occurs when a dream itself presents it.

Heroes are people who move out and accomplish something (perhaps a rescue). In our opinion there is a difference in the psychology of males and females, but we are unable to detect any difference for males and females in the basic pattern of the hero journey as reflected in the inner journey of spiritual growth. As noted earlier, *hero* as we use it in this book denotes a person moving toward some courageous achievement, but not the macho, swaggering gunman disregarding others in an individualistic push for ascendancy over them.

Having said that, does any difference remain between the experience of women's and men's journeys? The entire area of the psychological differences (if any) between men and women is a difficult one to pin down. The raising of consciousness about our stereotypical thinking which has resulted from the women's movement has begun to free both women and men from the limitations of trying to be someone different in order to "fit." Yet during these transitional times, when both men and women struggle to discover new ways of being, it becomes problematical to describe what is meant by "masculine" and "feminine." Almost any description is likely to offend someone.

Lists of characteristics attributed to masculinity and femininity are offered and shot down in sometimes vitriolic exchanges. Arguments also continue over whether traditional associations with the genders are inherent or culturally imposed. They will probably continue for some time, since it is difficult to see how one can sufficiently evade the context of one's own culture to make a definitive assessment about any possible ontological basis.

Though he lived before much of the contemporary work of consciousness raising in the women's movement, Jung has been the focus of some of the arguments, largely because of his theory of the "animus" and "anima." These figures (which Jung, as always in his theoretical constructs, claimed he had discovered empirically in dreams and unconscious material) are the contrasexual components of human personality.

In other words, just as each person has a minority of genes in the body which are associated with the other gender, Jung felt that each person has a psychological component associated with the opposite gender—women having a masculine part which Jung called animus and men having a feminine part which he called anima. In dreams, figures of the opposite sex are seen as animus or anima figures.

Jung felt that these figures play a distinctive role in one's personality. For one thing, they operate at a "deeper layer" in the unconscious and thus have, as one important function, the relationship of the conscious ego to the profound center of each person, which Jung called the "Self." In this role, such personifications serve to guide the conscious person to questions of the meaning of life. To put this in Jungian terminology, the anima and animus help each person connect to the Self. Self images are portrayed in dreams by god images or other images of wholeness.

Jung postulated that such contrasexual images in the psyche have both personal and archetypal or universal sources. The parents of the opposite sex and other formative people in the personal life shape the animus and anima. Cultural history (both of the particular racial and national group and of humankind as a whole) has also associated certain tasks and traits with each gender. Whatever physiological differences there are, of course, also shape the ideation of masculine and feminine. All of these are seen as sources of animus and anima.

Though Jung did not live to take part in the current discussions and arguments about masculine and feminine, he would, it seems obvious, take the position that the traditional associations have *psychological* significance for human development, whatever the source of the associations.

An example of one of the better attempts from within Jungian thought to suggest clusters of meaning which attach to "feminine" and "masculine" is in John Sanford's *The Invisible Partners*. This useful book presents Jung's theory of these components of personality in clear language. Sanford differentiates masculine and feminine by focusing on images rather than psychological functioning: "To speak of male and female is a way of saying that psychic energy, like all forms of energy, flows between two poles. Just as electricity flows between a positive and a negative pole, so psychic energy flows between two poles that have been called masculine and feminine."[1]

Sanford then uses the ancient Chinese terminology of yang and yin and the imagery associated with these terms:

> Yang means "banners waving in the sun," that is, something "shone upon" or bright. Yang is designated by heaven, the sky, the bright, the creative, the south side of the mountain (where the sun shines) and the north side of the river (which also receives the sunlight). On the other hand, in its primary meaning Yin is "the cloudy, the overcast." Yin is designated by the earth, the dark, the moist, the receptive, the north side of the mountain and the south side of the river. Of course the Chinese also speak of Yang as the masculine and Yin as the feminine, but basically Yang and Yin represent the two spiritual poles along which all life flows.[2]

As effective an attempt as this is to be fair-minded, the list is still irritating to feminists. Jean has commented that she doesn't like being relegated to all the shadowy, uncreative imagery through her feminine nature even if it is ancient.

When the actual hero stories are examined, though, some of this difficulty is avoided. It is intersting to note, for example, that Campbell's first story of a hero journey is the fairy tale of the Frog King.

Though it is named, as are many other tales, for the enchanted person who is rescued from the curse, the person in the story upon whose growth and maturity the tale is focused is the king's daughter. More often than many realized, women have been heroes—from Gretel to the English folk song hero Grace Darling, who saved the drowning sailors.

The Septuagint Book of Judith contains one of the clearest hero tales in Scripture. There, as the leaders of the city quiver in fright, ready to surrender to the attacking Holofernes, Judith reminds them that capture will mean the destruction of Jerusalem and is therefore apostasy. She goes forth to Holofernes and slays him in the midst of his drunkenness and lust, thereby freeing the city.

Diane Apostolos-Cappadona puts it well when she says that in Judith the traditional story of the beautiful damsel in distress has become the beautiful damsel who saves a city in distress. Apostolos-Cappadona traces the fascinating changes in artistic representations of Judith through the centuries. Judith became a popular symbol of liberty and freedom against civil tyranny. For Christian artists, she also became the inverse of Salome, who was responsible for the beheading of the good prophet John the Baptist, with Judith and Salome representing virtue and vice. Judith evidently was more an artistic projection of the then-current view of women than she was an accurate portrayal as she appears in Scripture. This is notable in post-Reformation Protestant artists, who began to portray her nude and as a temptress, contrary to the text itself.[3]

A modern artistic portrayal is the cantata *Judith,* the combined work of several women artists, which premiered at the National Conference of Christians and Jews in 1981. Insight into the modern relevance of Judith was caught both in the citing of an Auschwitz martyr and in the repeated refrain "[The] story is not in the end. . . . The story is in the going." This is elaborated at the end in the lines "The story is in the going where you have to go / to be true, to be true to your name."[4] Perhaps Judith is coming back into her own as a symbol of female heroism. The cantata emphasizes the difficulty of going on the heroic journey, never knowing how it will end, only knowing that one must be true to oneself, to one's vocation.

Female heroes abound in literature and have been identified, traced, and explicated.[5] Whatever differences there may be in women's and men's hero journeys, contrary to what some theorists say, women do go on hero journeys and bring back treasures. The hero journey is not necessarily misogynist.

One of the most interesting suggestions of the way in which women take hero journeys has been described by Mara Donaldson.[6] Using Campbell's monomyth pattern of separation-initiation-return as a background, she suggests that the woman's hero journey is different from the man's hero journey in the nature of its movement. She says that the male journey begins in arrogance or hubris and that the hero, to achieve his goal, must move toward a self-achieved submission, humility, or self-awareness. She sees this as the customary usage of "hero journey."

In contrast, she says the woman's journey begins in submission, humiliation, or humility (her customary position in the culture) and moves toward self-affirmation. Thus, she urges that to begin to understand the norms of women's journeys, the world must stop interpreting the woman's journey in terms of the mans's—must listen anew to women's stories, especially those that move toward self-affirmation.

Arguments similar to those of Donaldson are made by feminists about the psychology of the human ego. Demaris Wehr, for example, objects to Jung's belief (and I presume to those of other psychologists who share his ego emphasis) that individuation starts with an assumption of an ego which believes itself to be master in its own house. Wehr says this theory is more applicable to men than to women, because women are less likely than men to have a sense of ego mastery.[7] Again, Jung knew and taught this, but Wehr is right in calling attention to his lack of clarity on this point.

As Wehr comments, this connects interestingly with the arguments of some women theologians about the nature of sin. Valerie Saiving Goldstein, for example, challenges the theological assertion that identifies sin with self-asssertion and love with selflessness.[8] Women, she says, are far more likely to fail to realize their full self-identity than they are to assert it inappropriately. She therefore calls for a new look at the definition of sin.

Ann Ulanov affirms Goldstein on sin from a woman's point of view: "For a woman sin is not pride, an exaltation of self, but a refusal to claim the self God has given. Women refuse this self by hiding behind self-doubt and feelings of inadequacy. The force of her [Goldstein's] argument arises from countless women's experience of avoiding the self that they are, by always assuming that some greater authority knows better, be that father, mother, husband, even, in this case, theolgians' interpretation of sin."9

These are compelling arguments, and they resonate with many women's experience. It is certainly time to listen to women's stories, yet the strict division between men and women about hero journeys (and about sin) seems to us not to hold up when applied to the life experience of actual women and men.[10] In addition to the people who resonate with these categories, there are also women who begin in hubris and need the move toward humility, and there are men who begin in humility and need the move toward self-affirmation. Further, a person who needs humility at one time in life may well need self-affirmation at another. These variations are true not only of the stories of men and women today, but also of the myths and folk and fairy tales.

Donaldson does call attention, however, to an important truth—all hero stories are not the same; there is great individuality in them, despite their general monomyth shape. It probably is also true that there is a generalized pattern, which might appropriately be called a "masculine" journey, which moves from hubris to humility, and that there is another generalized pattern, which might appropriately be called a "feminine" journey, which moves from humility to self-affirmation. Both kinds of journey can be needed by both men and women. Both kinds of journey can also be experiences of spiritual growth, though the journey toward humility is frequently taught as the only appropriate journey. Donaldson's theory broadens our view of the heroic journey and suggests a typology of journeys which may well be helpful in assessing and understanding the journey one is engaged in.

Another helpful typology of hero journeys is that of Carol Pearson. She identifies six different heroic archetypes people experience at different stages of life: the Innocent, the Orphan, the Wanderer, the Warrior, the Martyr, and the Magician. Citing Carol Gilligan's developmental work, Pearson suggests that women and men tend to develop the varied archetypes in a different order. She postulates that some generalizations about gender seem to hold up, though she recognizes that men and women "do not always and inevitably experience these stages in different orders."[11]

Though these typologies are helpful, the study of them seems to us to point even more to what we have come to believe is the major emphasis of human growth: the *individual* nature of each person's journey. It is obvious that each person is different from others, yet when theorists begin to generalize, it is easy to lose sight of this obvious truth. As one of our teachers used to say, "These theories are very helpful, as long as you don't think they are *true*."

An interesting visual view of the journey comes with Joseph Campbell's emphasis on the circular aspect of the hero journey (departure-initiation-return), as in the illustrative diagram in Chapter 2. Yet a straight line is what most people picture when growth is spoken of as a "journey" or "path." Because the nature of the hero journey is circular as well as linear and sometimes repetitive, it is probably best represented by a spiral. The shape of the patterns of growth will appear most clearly in the dream examples in the remainder of the book.

The linear aspect emphasizes the action and forward movement, and the circular aspect emphasizes that the return of the hero involves coming back to the same place again. Both come together in the spiral aspect, which emphasizes that no one engages in only one heroic journey through life. Many heroic journeys are required throughout life, and each one in a sense leaves from the same "place" and returns to it again. The difference is what the heroes *become* in the journey, as they themselves are changed.

This movement of going round and round and also moving forward reminded one seminar participant of the structure of DNA—the material (protein) which forms the active substance of genes and the code for genetic transmission. He pointed out that this is formed as a helix, a structure similar to a spring. Perhaps there is an association between these two things that operate as the basis of life—the code allowing for cell reproduction and the monomyth pattern of ongoing development of the psyche.[12] Perhaps the linear view of development—ever onward and upward—is a more masculine orientation and the circular more feminine. The spiral or helix may fit more comfortably with both feminine and masculine by combining the linear (traditionally and physically associated with the masculine) and the circular (traditionally and physically associated with the feminine).

To summarize, we think both women and men go on hero journeys several times during their lives—each time, in fact, that a new task, test, or increment of learning is to be achieved. We are using the hero journey in a gender-free manner, without attempting to define the nature of a given person's journey at a given time in life. Clues can be used from developmental theory and from feminist theory, but not in a normative way. The hero journey in the service of inner growth does not simply follow any linear, lock-step, developmental path.

# ▶5

# Understanding Dreams

Jung's theory of how to understand dreams is a phenomenological one; he viewed the dream itself as a phenomenon. He stressed taking each dream on its own terms and trying from that beginning to decode its symbolism. In doing so he looked first at the dreamer's own associations with the images. He called this process "personal amplification."

Yet he also postulated from his experience working with dreams that there are general motifs which go beyond the personal and can illumine dreams. How can this be true? How can people's dreams have motifs from beyond their personal experience?

In truth no one knows the answer to these questions with certainty. Once one grants that such occurrences exist, though, a theory to explain them is needed. In ancient times and on through the medieval period the subject of dream interpretation was given considerable attention.[1] In this century only depth psychology and spiritual directors have explored the question of how to understand dreams.

Jung postulated that there is a deeper "layer" than personal history in the psyche and named that layer the "collective unconscious." He called the contents of the collective unconscious "archetypes," or primordial patterns of human behavior. Of course, such primordial patterns were already inherent in Freud's observations of the "archaic remnants" in personality, but Jung broadened the study of such factors far beyond the sexual, on which Freud had focused.

The theory of the collective unconscious lends itself to placing emphasis on the study of stories and patterns such as the monomyth. The study of these general fields of human knowledge is a major thrust of Jungian dream work. Adding information from such fields is the process Jung called "general amplification." General associations enlarge the understanding of the possible significance of dream symbols.

Another of Jung's theories is that dreams are *compensatory* to the conscious attitude of the dreamer. In other words, the dream is a kind of "snapshot" of the psyche, holding up in symbolic language the ignored or neglected part of the picture. For example, when the dreamer is too one-sided or exaggerated in some view, the dream may show a picture of an exaggerated or one-sided stance in the opposite direction. Dreams thus hold up the dreamer's blind spots.

Jung felt that most dreams dealt with one's inner attitude toward life, and thus most dreams portray in dramatic form various parts of the dreamer's attitudes. Human beings tend to be not one, but a whole committee of conflicting views, desires, fears, and attitudes; and dreams act out these tensions and potentialities symbolically. Thus Jung felt that most of the people and other images in dreams represented parts of the dreamer. He called this the *subjective* understanding of dream images. Occasionally dreams refer to the dreamer's relation to some known person in the outer world and so make sense with an *objective* interpretation; but this occurs less often. We will follow this theory in most of the interpretations in this book, though sometimes both the objective and subjective interpretations of a dream figure will be explored.

Jung also believed that several dreams in a series were more helpful than a single dream. With a series, one could observe the changes in attitude and developments in behavior. We have discovered that this is very important in working with the monomyth as an interpretive aid to dream work. In Part III, we will present several dream series to illustrate how this can be informative, as one dream develops the themes in a former one. We have also found that to interpret dreams with the monomyth pattern it is necessary to know more of the dreamer's life situation than was absolutely necessary in our former writing about dream interpretation. We therefore tend to tell more of the dreamers' stories than we did in *Symbols of Transformation in Dreams*.

For more details about the general interpretation of dreams, we refer readers to that book and to others cited in the suggested readings listed there. We trust, however, that with this brief introduction to dream theory, even those unfamiliar with the interpretive process will be able to understand the examples which follow.

One of the ways a hero motif is announced in a dream is that a figure who is clearly heroic appears in the dream, seemingly to point up the heroic quality of an action in which the dreamer is currently involved. Jean had such a dream shortly after we arrived in Zurich to study at the Jung Institute in 1964:

> At first there was Joan of Arc as Julie Harris played her—she was strong, but small in stature. I don't remember what she did.

When Jean took this dream to her analytical hour, her analyst thought a moment and then asked if she had recently taken any action without Wallace's knowledge. She was shocked by the question, since she had in fact secretly written a letter to the United States about money we would need to supplement our grant. The analyst laughed and commented that Joan of Arc went to war without the king of France!

The symbol "Joan of Arc" called to her attention, perhaps, the strength and independence of setting out on her own to handle a difficult situation. At the same time, the analyst's question raises the point that the situation is probably more appropriately handled as a joint decision. Jean thinks it probably also indicated her unconscious irritation with Wallace's failure (like that of the dauphin) to take action as fast as she thought he should—not an uncommon source of difference between extraverts like Jean and introverts like Wallace.

There is probably also an irony here. Jean's dream is not a dream of Saint Joan herself, but of an actress *playing* her. The dream may thus suggest that Jean is playing at being Joan of Arc. Such associations raise the issue again: should the secret be maintained? Jean decided that it should not, and the money problem was jointly handled after that.

To review the procedure used to interpret this dream, the action which takes place in the dream is observed. Here there is little—only an image. An actress plays the role of an actual historical character. The actual historical character is an obviously heroic person. The analyst reflected on the historical events around that character to explore what possible significance there could be in the dreamer's current life situation. Then he asked a question, and when he received an affirmative answer from Jean, the two of them (analyst and dreamer) were on the trail of discovery.

Jean could then make the connection between the historical character and the current events in her own life. The remainder of the commentary on the dream is a process of weighing the material from the unconscious which the heroic figure brings to light in order to see what commentary it makes on the dreamer's outer situation and inner attitudes. *Then,* with this new information, the dreamer can make a more conscious decision.

Another way heroic imagery is presented in dreams is as a depiction of heroic action. Here is a dream in which such action occurs and the action is labeled heroic within the dream itself:

> I dreamed I was skiing. The slope was rocky, with huge rocks and tree stumps showing. It was dangerous, and I was having a hard time maneuvering down the slope. I came across two people, a couple, who were buried beneath a fallen rock. I stopped, and there was a ski patrolman helping the couple. I told the patrolman that I was a nurse and could help. I rescued this couple, and they both survived. I was so happy and proud that I had saved someone's life. I felt like a hero.

This is the dream of a young wife and mother in her mid-thirties. She enjoyed skiing, so her personal amplification of skiing was positive. Furthermore, she was a nursing student, just about to graduate from her training. She had done well in her studies and internships and thus had experienced confirmation of her ability to be a nurse, as well as enjoyment and a sense of value in her chosen profession. All these personal associations suggest that the dream is picking up her sense of being a success to speak to her about some area of her life in which success may be achieved—in which she can feel "like a hero."

After identifying this feeling tone from the dream and the dreamer's personal amplification of its symbols, we turn to her life situation to compare it with the dream. What is going on in her life now for which the dream imagery might be suggesting this positive compensatory possibility?

The dream came at a difficult time in her life. Her husband had moved away from home, leaving her and the children. For the first time in her life, she was forced to function as a single parent, as the only responsible adult in her family. She wanted to save her marriage and thought marriage counseling might help, but efforts in that direction had thus far been unsuccessful. Her husband had refused to commit to marriage counseling, and the future of their marriage was uncertain.

Though all this was distressing to her, she had at the same time experienced a sense of relief from the separation. She became aware that the relationship had become very destructive. If they did continue in the marriage, some changes needed to be made. She was also finding, to her surprise, that she could function without her husband, something she had never thought possible.

With this background, a connection with the dream can be made. The setting at the beginning portrays their situation visually. The terrain is rocky and dangerous, and she is having a hard time. The couple "buried beneath a fallen rock" probably represent her and her husband; Jungians would call them a "shadow couple."

The dream then points up that help is available to the "fallen" couple. There is an unknown male helper in the person of the ski patrolman, probably an animus of the dreamer, a masculine part of herself. There is also the dreamer herself in the dream, pictured as a nurse-helper. The dream says she is able to rescue this couple, to save their lives, and in the dream she rejoices in that strength and ability.

In the dream she can experience the happiness of being a hero, despite the opposite way she is feeling in outer life. Since dreams carry the compensatory energy, the dream itself can help her go on with that task of maneuvering through the dangerous, rocky slope. The portrayal in the dream of the rescue of the couple, their survival, and her happiness at her ability to help—all bode well for her ability to handle whatever life presents her with, perhaps even their survival as a couple.

Significantly, it is *her* efforts which the dream shows as rescuing the couple. She had felt that it was her husband who needed to rescue them, but the dream says she has a hero journey to take in order to save the couple. The dream throws the responsibility on her, while at the same time holding out encouraging imagery of success.

Even when the heroic connection is not as clear as it is in these two dreams, the individual motifs or "keys" may identify a part of her hero journey, or the refusal of the journey, to the dreamer. We will explore these parts of the journey in the next section.

# Part II
# Hero Motifs in Dreams

*We can distinguish three elements of life: self-identity, self-alteration, and return to one's self.*

*Paul Tillich*

# ▶6
# The Call to Adventure

The vocational summons or call to adventure may come in a variety of ways: a seeming accident changes the home situation, a foreign visitor arrives unexpectedly, one hears of a golden ring that must be recovered, a dragon has the land in thrall, one sees a burning bush that is not consumed by the fire, or one's jealous brothers sell one into slavery. Adventure stories provide many examples.

We have found no better story than the one Joseph Campbell used to introduce his discussion of the call to adventure: the Grimm fairy tale of the Frog King. The story tells of a king's youngest daughter who was very beautiful. One day she went into the dark forest near the castle and sat down under an old tree beside a spring. Since she was bored, she started to play with her favorite toy, a golden ball. After one throw it did not fall back into her little hand but rolled into the water, which was very deep.

The little girl began to cry loudly, but stopped when she heard someone ask why she was crying. Much to her surprise she found it was a frog. When she told him about losing her golden ball, the frog offered to recover it for her but asked what she would give him for doing so. The little girl quickly offered her clothes, her jewels, and even the crown she was wearing. The frog said he was not interested in those items, but if she would love him and be his companion and let him sit at her table, eat off her plate, drink out of her cup, and sleep in her bed, then he would go down below and bring up her golden ball.

The little girl quickly promised him everything he wanted, but thought to herself that he was foolish to think a frog could be a close companion of a princess, so her promise did not matter. As soon as he brought up the ball and tossed it on the grass, the little girl grabbed it up and ran away toward home. The frog begged her to wait for him, since he could not run so fast, but she paid no attention.

The next day when she was at table with her father the king, there was a knocking at the door and a voice calling out for the princess to open it. She opened the door, but when she saw the frog she slammed it shut. The king asked why she was so frightened, and after hearing the story of the frog told her she must keep her promises. One by one the frog requested the fulfillment of each of her promises. Finally, in the bedroom, when the frog asked to be put into her bed and threatened to tell her father if she did not do so, she picked him up in disgust and threw him against the wall. When the frog landed he was no longer a frog but a handsome prince who told her that he had been bewitched and no one could have delivered him from the spell but herself. The next day, he said, they would go together to his kingdom. So, as in good fairy tales, there is a happy ending; something has been accomplished, and the story is over.

In this fairy tale there are several signs or indications that something is about to happen to the little princess. She has played with the ball many times, and no doubt had dropped it before but had picked it up without further ado. This time the ball disappears, and a frog appears and talks. The little girl makes some ill-considered promises. She has been drawn into an adventure; things are about to change. The little girl has been asleep, you might say, and events are going to force her to *wake up* (if she can). To carry this further, symbolically, you could say the "father principle" in her wins out and she learns to be faithful to her promises. She did not *choose* to go on the adventure of transformation, but her own boredom was a factor in the call.

The opening scene has a number of typical symbols such as those one might find in a dream, and these symbols can be amplified in stories as they are in dreams. There is a dark forest, suggesting perhaps an unconscious state, as light symbolically suggests consciousness. There is a spring. All of life comes out of water; and water from a spring is continually being renewed and changed, which may suggest the possibility of renewal and change for the princess. The ball itself, being round—and important, since it is golden—is a symbol of wholeness. Circles seem to represent wholeness at a natural, unconscious level. They are complete, without beginning or end.

Now, suddenly, the princess can only regain that symbol of wholeness through the offices of a loathsome frog. The loathsome creature varies in stories, but it is frequently something one would normally reject. Acceptance of something unacceptable is a required motif. That which is a part of oneself but of which one is unaware often seems unacceptable.

In the story the little girl foolishly makes a promise to a loathsome frog. She has something to learn and to accept. There is an inner principle that needs to be obeyed (the father king), and she has to learn to accept the responsibility of living up to principles of truth and integrity. And further, there is a part of herself (the frog) that has been rejected and that must be accepted. In the story she reluctantly, but nevertheless faithfully (because of the king's orders), begins to do the things required and the spell is broken. The little girl had something to learn: the possibility of an increase of consciousness was being presented. She was about to leave childhood and become an adult. It is interesting that in the story it is at the moment when she exercised some independence, some resolution of conflicting pressures within (when she throws the frog against the wall), that the spell is broken. The union with the prince (the story's conclusion) suggests that the inner integration has been completed.

In story, as C. S. Lewis says, "The imagined beings have their insides on the outside; they are visible souls."[1] The process of *inner* development is presented to the reader as characters and situations on the outside.

The call to adventure may even come by way of *curiosity*, which rings up the curtain on the drama to follow. Moses, the great hero of the Israelites, was started on his last journey this way. John Sanford calls Moses "the reluctant hero."[2] In the biblical story Moses is tending his flock when he sees a bush that is burning but is not being consumed by the fire. Out of curiosity Moses goes to investigate and encounters his God, who calls him to a task of setting his people free.

To do so he must do battle with the mighty pharaoh of Egypt. Moses is appropriately reluctant, argues with God, but loses the argument. He chooses, finally, to follow God, and his adventure has begun.

Sometimes a tragedy can signal the call to adventure. Then it may seem that the hero has no choice, but, even so, there is still the choice of the hero's response to the tragedy. The noted Viennese psychiatrist Viktor Frankl was a death camp survivor. His father, mother, brother, and wife all died in the camps, and everything he possessed was lost. He suffered from hunger, cold, brutality, and the constant threat of death. With all outer identity removed, Frankl reports that "the last of the human freedoms" was all that remained—the ability to "choose one's attitude in any given set of circumstances, to choose one's own way."[3] Frankl chose to respond to this experience by the further development of his understanding of the human personality. His school of logotherapy stresses a basic human will-to-meaning. His "call to adventure" was conceived and executed in horror and through no personal choice; nevertheless, the choice remained to him to respond with courage and creativity.

Two popular films of the 1980s begin the hero's journey from the response made to tragedy. In *Star Wars*, Luke Skywalker longs to be a Jedi knight, without much idea of what that means. His uncle refuses to let him leave the farm, but when everyone else is killed while Luke is away one day, the tragedy plus the longing of his own heart send him off on his lifelong adventure against the Evil Empire. (George Lucas, the creator of *Star Wars*, said he based the *Star Wars* films on Campbell's hero book.)

In *Places of the Heart*, the young widow's hero adventure begins with the senseless death of her husband, followed by the threatened loss of her farm. Something in her responds with a determination to become someone new in order to save the farm, even in the face of all the doubts of the banker and the community.

The *Wizard of Oz* is a fine example of many different reasons to begin the journey. Dorothy is flung into Oz by a storm and only wants to get home. Each of the characters who joins her journey does so because of some lack he senses in himself. Each thinks that someone else or magic or the Wizard can provide what is missing, but each one finds that the help to become someone new comes from within.

In many hero stories, an inner "dream" or longing of the heart is a part of realizing the call to adventure. As we have suggested, sometimes a real sleeping dream in the night has images that signal a call, which the dreamer then has the choice to accept or reject.

### London Stopover

One humorous call to adventure came to a married woman about forty years old:

> I'm in a hotel room in London on a stopover. I have 24 hours before I leave and am trying to decide what to do. The hotel room is small and dark—the window is painted over with dark brown paint, so I can't see out. I can't think of how to spend my time—where to go, what to do. I try to think of the times we've visited London before. All the nuisance of figuring out the bus lines, tube lines, etc. I shouldn't miss this opportunity but I can't get focused. Now if I were only gorgeous I could just walk outside and something exciting would happen without my having to plan it at all. Then I look in the mirror and think, oh, well, what the hell, why not try it?

The movement of the story is clear. She is in a foreign country—not completely strange, but sufficiently confusing to create some anxiety. She is in a limited, dull place—imagine being in a small, strange hotel room with the window painted brown! She is torn between longing for adventure and opportunity on the one hand and fear and hesitation on the other. She lacks *focus* and longs to be gorgeous so someone would rescue her from having to make her own plans.

The most interesting point is that this is the dream of a sophisticated, intellectual woman, who would certainly have viewed herself as "above" such passivity. She saw herself, accurately, as a liberated professional. Yet at the time of the dream she was caught in an unpleasant office situation which upset her plans, perhaps even threatened her job, and she felt helpless in the face of that threat. The dream seems to indicate to her that she is a lot more eager to be rescued than she had thought, but it also encourages her to begin making her own plans and handling the situation on her own.

The combination of the dream's setting in the dismal room and her longing to respond to the opportunity of the stopover in London constitutes her call to adventure. The ending is not only an encouragement, but even perhaps an indication that the courage to answer the call lies within her, maybe just below the surface. The light quality of the dream suggests a good outcome if she does take charge, instead of staying in the passive place where she now finds herself.

### Separation from the Mother

A college student told us a dream he remembered from when he was about ten years old. He called it "the most memorable of my childhood":

> I am walking with my mother in a park on a path that borders alongside a pond. It is a very beautiful park with lots of singing birds and white swans floating gracefully on the pond. I am just a little boy, probably about 4 or 5. My mother is holding my hand quite tightly so I don't wander off by myself and get lost. I think this is quite strange that she is worried that I will run away because I am quite content and happy by her side.
>
> Suddenly, she loses her balance and slides down the embankment into the pond which suddenly transforms into a murky swamp. She disappears into the swamp almost instantaneously with only the bubbles of her last breath to mark her presence in the dark water. I try to save her by running down the embankment and reaching my arm into the swamp. But it is too late. All I can do is stand helpless and crying, wishing that she wouldn't have let go of my hand so I could have gone with her.

Though the dreamer no longer remembered the precise details of his life at the time of the dream, the dream gives us many internal clues about his life situation then. The opening scene of the dream contrasts with the desolate, limited imagery at the beginning of the other dreams above. Here he is in a park, happily enjoying its beauty with his mother. All appears to be well, except for the fact that he is a much younger boy in the dream than he was in waking life. Perhaps the dream suggests that he is behaving in a way that is too young for his age and that his mother is also behaving toward him in a way more appropriate to a four- or five-year-old than a ten-year-old. Maybe she is holding on to him too tightly, and maybe he is a bit too contented with staying by her side. Ten is a time for more adventure than the dream-ego appears to be ready for.

So perhaps we should not be surprised that the pleasant scene suddenly turns to horror. Not only does his mother fall, but the pond itself changes its nature. From a pond with graceful white swans, it is transformed into a swamp. When a parent clings too long, the relationship to the child does seem to take on the qualities of a murky swamp. Fairy tales represent this by giving the hero of the tale not a "true mother," but a "wicked stepmother." This imagery brings pain to many fine stepmothers, but it probably arises from the effort to express symbolically that it is *not* appropriate mothering for a child to remain too closely identified with the mother beyond the age when close care is needed for protection.

Life presents this dreamer with a change which the little boy feels incompetent to cope with. He even wishes he could have gone with her into the dark waters. This shocking image seems to come to the little boy at the time when the call of adolescence to move toward adulthood comes to him. The dream gives no clues as to his response.

### Fighting a Snake

Separation from the mother is also the theme of two dreams and some active imagination for a dreamer we will call Craig. Craig was a thirty-three-year-old psychotherapist whose girl friend, an older woman, broke off their relationship, though he begged her not to leave. He was in such pain that he could not eat for five days. The separation seemed to evoke his other losses of relationships; his first financée had died before their marriage, and his wife had divorced him. Though both of these were terrible experiences that took a long time to heal, he felt his current desertion as the greatest pain he had ever known.

As a result of this pain and his attempts to work through it, he came to understand that the relationship had failed in part because he was not reliable. He resisted growing up, taking adult responsibility; in short, he had never left his mother.

A helper with knowledge of American Indian practice (in which Craig was deeply interested) helped him in active imagination to experience a Sioux initiation ceremony called a Sundance, designed to help boys become men. They are hung until they have a vision in the midst of their pain. This ceremony comes before marriage so that the men won't "marry their mother."

Then he heard a lecture on masculine and feminine by Jungian analyst Marian Woodman, after which he dreamed a long and powerful dream with three major events. In the first scene, he was in a large banquet hall with a number of men and women, all dressed in tuxedoes and formal gowns, seated at U-shaped tables. Into the midst of this group of people, mostly middle-aged or older, came a blond woman his age dressed in a very revealing manner. All the women wanted her to leave, and Craig felt drawn to defend her.

Then suddenly a snake sixty feet long was on the other side of the table from Craig. The snake said, "This is my turf," and lunged forward to bite Craig. He was frightened. Everything seemed to happen in slow motion; he picked up a cafeteria tray and, using it as shield, barely moved fast enough to avoid the strike. He had a sense that the snake spoke first as a female, but then soon became masculine. He also felt the snake could have killed him had it wanted to.

Then the scene shifted outside to a swimming pool. Craig grabbed the snake and pulled part of him into the pool. The snake was so big Craig could barely wrap his arms around his neck. After a long struggle he thought he had killed the snake, but someone mentioned what all the men seemed to know: "The Mother Snake living in the cave would simply take one of the many small snake tails which were crawling all over her; it would grow a head and come after me again."

This is a very complicated dream, only parts of which we will examine, but it bears a striking resemblance to the battles with serpents which are a part of many hero stories, such as those of Hercules and Beowulf. The serpent in the cave, Jung points out, is an image which often occurred in antiquity, where the serpent not only aroused fear, but also signified healing. In the depths of the water (the unconscious), guarded by the serpent or the dragon, is the mysterious treasure. The serpent must be overcome, yet at the same time the serpent-power itself is the treasure.[4]

Some of this same ambivalence was present in Craig's serpent, who could have killed him if it chose and who was somehow both female and male. Craig's own associations with the serpent were first with his mother; he said it felt like his mother telling him not to pay attention to another woman, for "this was her turf." As he reflected over the next week on this aspect of the dream, he reviewed times when his mother had been sexually and emotionally abusive to him.

He said his father was gone almost half of each year on the job, and Craig was his mother's "favorite" who "obviously took the place of my father."

With such a history, it seems probable that Craig had indeed "married his mother" in his relationships with women—that somehow his failure to be free from emotional entanglement with his mother kept him from growing to maturity. The unknown blond woman was probably an anima figure; one of the tasks with which the anima can help a man is freeing himself from his mother so that he can form appropriate relationships with women.

Yet Craig also came to believe that the snake in its masculine form represented "my own power, which I must reclaim and own myself." He said further reflection on his feeling tone at the end of the dream showed him that the snake had let him think he had killed it "almost as if he was smiling, the smile of a loving father who has just allowed his son to beat him at wrestling or chess." This aspect of the dream made Craig wonder, "Perhaps this is my turf."

It is in this ambivalent sense that Jung discusses the hero and the dragon. The hero, he points out, has much in common with the dragon he fights, or rather, "he takes over some of its qualities." Thus, "the treasure which the hero fetches from the dark caverns is *life*: it is himself, new-born from the dark maternal cave of unconscious. . . . The hero who clings to the mother is the dragon, and when he is reborn from the mother he becomes the conqueror of the dragon." Jung also notes that the "hero is himself the snake, himself the sacrificer and the sacrificed."[5]

All this material was calling Craig to a hero journey, which the end of the dream seemed to show he was engaging in. Yet his own continuing pain, together with the hopeless warning at the end of the dream that he would have to fight this serpent again and again, were discouraging to him. At that point he had the following dream:

> Several nights later I had a short dream in which I was in the same room, empty of people. The white tables formed a perfect square, and I was standing in the middle. I had the cafeteria tray shield on my right arm and said, "Here I stand. If you want to fight me, come here. Here is where I choose to fight."

This dream gave Craig another boost of "en-courage-ment" to delve heroically and deeply into the unconscious material concerning his relation with his mother, so that he could truly separate from her and become the responsible adult person he was called to be.

## Escape from Prison

Sometimes a dream reveals to the dreamer that a lack of freedom imprisons her in ways of which she is unaware. The imagery can suggest that escape is possible, as in this dream:

> My father is holding me a prisoner. I am not free. I am confined to a small closet in a bedroom. But I am trying to escape. I know of a difficult secret passage down through a chest of drawers. I start to escape by rummaging through the clothes. Suddenly, he is there, so I quickly cover up my "progress" and act "cool." I pretend I was taking a nap on the bed. Dad is putting on his socks and talking to me. We are friendly. But I fear his "power."

This is a dream of a nun in her forties after four months of therapy, which she had entered for several reasons. She was in a time of transition, wondering whether she should continue in her previous profession of teaching or whether she should follow a new path. A change of direction would require more study, which her order had encouraged her to do. Yet she seemed blocked from the new roads in ways she did not understand, and it was this sense of being unable to make a decision either way which convinced her to seek help.

In working with this dream, she said she was not really in any regular contact with her father, so she had no sense that he as an actual person was still holding her the prisoner of his power. The father in the dream, then, represents some inner imprisoning power which makes her afraid—much the way the king in fairy tales represents the masculine power principle in the fairy tale kingdom.

In her case, this internalized fear probably had a number of sources. She had always been a "dutiful daughter" at home, and she had continued that practice in her religious order. Many women also become aware that the stereotype the culture teaches about women requires them to be submissive and obedient in order to be considered "good women." All these patterns, personal and cultural, probably contributed to her blockage.

During this period of her life, she was supposedly working on an educational plan to present to her order. This would involve finding out what schools and programs were available, how much they would cost, how well they would train her for new work, and so on. In fact she had taken no action at all. She blamed her lack of action on others—on how busy her institutional job kept her and on her lack of a private place from which to make telephone calls for information during office hours. Yet just before this dream, she had stayed home all day long during an unexpected "snow day" and had not made one telephone call. She said this was because she "had to do so much work to be ready" for the next day of work!

Actually, her own failure to take action on that snow day (when action was clearly possible to her, despite her protestations) and this dream forced her to see the truth that she was in fact afraid to take the risk of moving on in her life and instead kept putting off taking initiative for her future. Thus she scuttled the possibility of her own growth. In reflecting on this pattern, she began to recall with new understanding a number of areas each day in which she acted with the same fear and self-limiting behavior. She was truly being held a prisoner, but the prison was her own fear.

During the week which followed working with this dream, she reported that she became very angry with this pattern and all the limitation it implied. The anger somehow gave her new energy, and she was able in one week to begin the process she had put off for four months, though she found she had to fight a "battle" at almost every step of the way against an inner devaluing voice which would have denied she had any right to move forward in new ways with her life. By its limiting images of prison and pretense, the dream served as her call to new adventure and provided help by giving her the energy to carry through.

## An Autopsy

In the midst of a growing fear that he would die from cancer, a middle-aged man dreamed:

> All my family were at the place where we all grew up, and we seemed to be preparing for a party or celebration. We were all aware that Winnie was close to death. There was lots of activity like cleaning up, mowing lawns, and we were also breaking in some very fine looking Arab horses. Wally Lewis was there, and I was taking photos of him.

Eventually the news came through that Winnie had died, and I was expecting that they would bring the body there, but when it didn't arrive and I asked where it was, I was told it had been taken for a Post Mortem. I was upset about this, as I didn't think there was any need for her to be mutilated any more.

The dream includes many images from his actual life at the time. His friend Winnie had died of cancer two days before, and he himself was seriously concerned that he too had cancer, which would "beat" him. He had previously had five major operations for melanomas and skin cancers, and for about a year before the time of the dream he had developed stomach pains, which he feared were the first sign of a killing cancer.

The dreamer's life had been a tragic one. He had lost his parents and a sister early in life and two other siblings had died of cancer. He is an alcoholic who has been sober for ten years. Yet at the time of the dream some members of his family had blamed the family tragedies on his drinking: they said God had decided to take his siblings because of his drinking! Though he did not believe that was true, he felt very angry.

This anger, plus the fear of recurring cancer and the loss of his friend, had left him in bad shape. What does the dream say to this outer situation? The first startling thing we notice is that he and his family are back where they grew up, and they are all preparing to celebrate. He certainly was not feeling like celebrating in outer life, particularly with his family, so the dream presents him with a compensatory situation. Yet at the same time, the dream does not ignore his most recent sorrow, the death of Winnie.

When he gave his personal associations with his friend Winnie as a possible anima figure, he said Winnie represented to him the part of himself which had suffered deeply from the effects of cancer. They had shared this. As he put it, "To me she was a symbol of the mental and physical pain and the loneliness of the struggle, as her family hadn't been able to cope with the suffering she endured."

The image of Winnie was also significant with regard to his faith stance, just as the anima is frequently a man's guide to a deeper relationship with the Self or with God. Instead of agreeing with the critical members of the dreamer's family, who believed in tragedy as God's punishment, Winnie represented, he said, "the wholeness and maturity that comes from deep suffering." Winnie was a person who, like Viktor Frankl, had chosen to take an attitude toward suffering which gave the suffering meaning. If he integrated the Winnie-anima, the dreamer realized that he would then be able to trust God totally. Notice that Winnie does not represent a blind, clinging belief which thinks God will inevitably save him from death; Winnie had died two days before. Rather, the faith she represents for the dreamer is one which chooses God despite whatever happens.

In the dream, the family members are engaged in cleaning and sprucing up their home place. From some of the interaction mentioned above, it sounds as if there was a lot of cleaning up to be done in their destructive interactions. Whether the family is ready to clean things up in the outer world or not, the dream imagery shows them doing so—perhaps referring to the job the dreamer himself needs to do within, to clean up the remnants of these destructive attitudes left in him.

They were also breaking some very fine-looking Arab horses. This is a positive image of power. He was a horse trainer, and this image points perhaps to his learning to use this outward physical power in an adaptive way in his inner life.

Wally Lewis for him represented "the very positive and capable winner in me." The dreamer is an Australian from Queensland, and Wally Lewis is the Australian Rugby League Football captain—a sports legend in Queensland. For the dreamer, Lewis was a recognized "out and out winner," and "able to cope with all the pressures that go with being a winner." He himself had often felt like a loser. He felt the fact that he was taking photos of Wally Lewis in the dream meant that he needed to keep that positive winning shadow image before him.

We would add that dreaming of Winnie and Wally Lewis indicates that these qualities are also potentially present in his own life, so their appearance is a strong encouragement to him to relate more consciously to them. We also wonder if there is a pun involved in the dream. Just as Wally Lewis represented a "winner" to him, so his friend's name picked up this motif—"Winnie."

He related the postmortem to which Winnie was being subjected to his own fear of further mutilation from surgery. At the time he feared that he would need further face surgery, but it turned out that he did not need more major surgery. We think the dream may also suggest that he needs to dissect all that the symbol of his friend Winnie represents, so he can know what brought about the death—the general purpose of a postmortem. Though he resists the idea of the postmortem in the dream, in outer life he began to analyze the meaning of this and subsequent dreams with a counselor, an excellent step at such a frightening moment in his life. This dream of a party with Wally Lewis, the beautiful Arab horse, and the cleaning up of the family place are a call to go on the journey of getting to a different world view. Another dream of his described later in this book (in Chapter 11 under the title "Ripe for the Harvest") carries his story forward after he has gone through some of the *inner* postmortem involved in his journey.

## Call to a Parish

A dream which induced an Episcopal clergyman to change his mind about a *call* to a new parish came to him in the midst of a week of decision and confusion. He was in his late forties and had served his parish for over ten years as their rector when he received a formal call to become the rector of a church in another state—one he found most attractive.

He said he felt he had been responsible in considering the possible change. He had gone to visit the new church and really loved the people and the area of the country. He thought he had skills the church could use and furthermore thought his old parish was in good shape for him to leave.

He received the call on a Tuesday or Wednesday before the annual parish retreat, agonized over it during the retreat, and accepted the call on Monday. He then dictated a letter telling his parish that he was leaving, and the letter went out on Wednesday.

He reported feeling restless all that week, but could not understand why, because he wanted to go and had decided to do so. On Thursday night he dreamed:

> I had received the call and accepted it. I had told everyone. Then I changed my mind, told them I wasn't coming and told my vestry I wanted to come back. They said unfortunately they had hired someone else. My feeling of the thrust of the dream was the feeling of rejection.

The dream brought the whole matter into question for him again. He discussed it with his wife, who was not especially happy with the proposed move, and he continued generally to struggle with his sense of restlessness. Was he making a wrong decision? What was the right move for him?

At a vestry meeting on Saturday, he told them he was reconsidering, but only if they still wanted him. (Perhaps the dream had made him wary of assuming that he could come back!) The vestry said they did want him, and he then called the new parish and turned them down.

The incident was very embarrassing for him. He may be the only priest in America who told his congregation that he was staying with them because of a dream! The new parish had been notified that he was coming, and he kept receiving letters of welcome and congratulation. He had even filled out the information sheet for the new *Clerical Directory* that week, so he appeared in it as the rector of a church he never served.

He had read his dream as saying that his "call" was to stay where he was, but in the year that followed many things changed for him. It was a year of great pain and anger, which could fairly be considered a road of trials. Yet he felt that, though it would have been more pleasant in the new parish, the year was a learning experience for him.

He said, for example, that before the embarrassment of accepting and then changing his mind, he had felt "cocky." His image of himself was of a tightrope walker who managed to keep his balance. This experience took away his cockiness and left him with a lot of needed humility.

Then, about a year later, he was elected bishop in another diocese. It seems likely that he would not have felt good about leaving a new parish where he had served less than a year, even to accept election. Perhaps with the help of his dream he was being saved for a different call to adventure—one in which he could bring to the community of his new diocese the treasure of his new humility.

Phyllis Stark, wife of the former Episcopal Bishop of Newark, New Jersey, worried several years ago when her husband was first elected bishop. She explained her worry to him by saying she had noticed that bishops tended to do one of two things—they would either swell or grow—and she did not want a husband who would swell. The hero discussed above may have received his painful gift of humility to prepare him to be one of those who grows.

The journey always seems frightening at the beginning, the way almost always seems unclear, and of course the call can be misread or refused. There are, though, aids for the confused or reluctant hero to help cross the threshold. Some of them are discussed in the next chapter.

# ▶7
## Crossing the Threshold

When the call has come—however it comes—there is the problem of crossing the threshold. It takes courage; some find they have it and others do not. When the call is refused or left unanswered, the adventure turns into its negative. What seems to be a decision for security and the status quo may turn into a desert or wasteland of walled-in boredom, missed opportunities, and hard work without the expected rewards of energy well spent. The stories and folk tales make clear that what is usually involved in the refusal of the call is a refusal to give up what one takes to be one's own interest (sometimes in the guise of doing one's duty), and such calls come throughout life. The temptation is to choose the less adventurous way of comparatively unconscious group routines.

A particularly vivid image of the problems in leaving the home place and accepting the call is the biblical story of the rich young ruler who came to Jesus, asking what he must do to find eternal life. Jesus told him to keep the commandments. The ruler said he had done so since his youth and inquired, "What do I still lack?" This is a frequent component of the call; one's world feels incomplete—there must be more than this. Scripture says that Jesus looked at him and loved him and then issued the invitation to become one of his followers. The young ruler was grieved because he had great possessions and "went away sorrowful."

In stories, life, and dreams the call can be refused. In *Symbols of Transformation in Dreams* we discussed one symbol of the frightening quality of the unknown in our chapter on "Snakes." The snake, like the hero journey, can be dangerous, but (again like the hero journey) the snake is an archetype of transformation and renewal. In one of the dreams we told there a young woman in college was handed a snake by her girl friend. Though in her dream she and the friend "were supposed to do something with it," she refused and "it dropped on the floor with a thud." As we suggested there, some possibility of new awareness was being presented to her, but so far she was dropping it—with a thud.

People get the courage to accept the call in different ways. The story of Daniel from Hebrew Scripture tells of a young man who meets the challenge of a new demand, laid upon him involuntarily, with the resources of his religious tradition. This is an interesting motif because here faithfulness to tradition bolsters his courage in the new situation. The old song is sung in a new land.

His story begins with the capture of the kingdom of Judah by Nebuchadnezzar of Babylonia. Nebuchadnezzar ordered his chief aide to select some of the most noble and capable of the young men from among the captives of Judah and train them for three years to prepare them to serve in the royal court. They were to be given the best of everything, including the rich royal food and wine.

In order to be faithful and maintain his identity, Daniel resolved not to eat the royal food; in the language of today, he resolved to keep the kosher food laws. He even managed to persuade the king's aide that he would be just as strong and fit without eating the royal food. (Daniel would be a good model for today's proponents of health food; at the end of ten days he and his friends who ate vegetables were "better in appearance and fatter in flesh" than the youths who ate the king's rich food.) Daniel and his friends were afterward able to meet the challenges of many terrible situations by relying on their God and the observances of their tradition. Most Bible scholars today would understand the stories of Daniel and his friends as stories remembered in order to help build up the courage of the Israelites during their time of captivity and foreign oppression.

In the very human world of Scripture, another hero, Queen Esther, develops her courage due to mixed motives, as do most people. Esther was among the Jews living under the rule of the Persian empire. Her cousin Mordecai, who had adopted Esther, advised her to keep secret the fact that she was Jewish, and she had done so. The crisis came when one of the king's men plotted to have all Jews killed.

Because of Esther's position in the king's harem, Mordecai urged her to save her people by pleading with the king.

Esther sent him the message that anyone who approached the king without being sent for was summarily put to death. She wanted to help her people, but was afraid. Mordecai warned her in another message that she was no safer than they were if all Jews were killed. Then he added an encouraging appeal, citing such action as the possible meaning of her life: "And who knows whether you have not come to the kingdom for such a time as this?" Esther sent word that she would go, asking for prayers and fasting on her behalf, and she was able to save her people.

Her crossing of the threshold seems to have been achieved through a combination of threat (death will probably come if she doesn't), longing to save her people, resignation ("If I perish, I perish"), faith in God (prayer and fasting), and a sense of her purpose in life (being a queen so that she could save her people). Esther was not able to cross the threshold when she first faced it, but her courage was built up to the point where she could.

Peter in the New Testament is also someone who was not able to cross his threshold the first time. Even though he had been nicknamed the "rock" and forewarned about how hard it would be to stand by Jesus in the face of the threat of death, he still denied Jesus when the moment came. He could not take that fence. Yet after the resurrection he had another opportunity to respond, and he crossed many thresholds after that, repeatedly responding to the call "Feed my sheep."

One very old mode of achieving courage to move, which may sound odd to modern ears, is the boast or taunt. The heroes-in-the-making either boasted aloud about their ability or belittled their opponents with taunts. Such patterns always come to the fore in wartime.

Many scholars think that the oldest part of Scripture is a brief poem that contains such a boast. It is speculated that this poem, apparently irrelevant to the material around it, is a celebration of the invention of metal weapons. Whatever it celebrates, it is clearly a boast:

> Lamech said to his wives:
> "Adah and Zillah, hear my voice;

> you wives of Lamech, hearken to what I say:
> I have slain a man for wounding me,
> a young man for striking me.
> If Cain is avenged sevenfold,
> truly Lamech seventy-sevenfold."[1]

The night before a battle to be fought against great odds Shakespeare's most heroic king, Henry V, speaks to his soldiers in stirring words which have become justly famous. When an aide wishes for ten thousand more men for the coming battle, Shakespeare's King Henry chides him, saying, "The fewer men, the greater share of honor," adding that the battle fought the next day shall bring such fame that:

> And gentlemen in England now abed
> Shall think themselves accursed they were not here,
> And hold their manhoods cheap whiles any speaks
> That fought with us upon Saint Crispin's day.[2]

Interestingly, Laurence Olivier made a movie of this stirring play in England during World War II, with omissions of the sections which were less overtly heroic. The old words were used anew to inspire the English with courage to fight against great odds.

The wartime prime minister of England, Winston Churchill, was famous for his inspirational speeches in the dark days of that war. During the Battle of Britain, for instance, he said to his people:

> Therefore we must regard the next week or so as a very important period in our history. It ranks with the days when the Spanish Armada was approaching the Channel, and Drake was finishing his game of bowls; or when Nelson stood between us and Napoleon's Grand Army at Boulogne. We have read all about this in the history books; but what is happening now is on a far greater scale and of far more consequence to the life and future of the world and its civilization than those brave old days.[3]

Notice that each of the preceding quotes includes a glance at history, either personal, tribal, or national. The speaker in each instance places himself and those who are allied with him within the context of a history they share. He offers a perspective beyond the present fear. One speaker says, in effect, think how it will be in future times to know yourself identified with this bravery. Another recalls high moments in the nation's history from the past (all of which, of course, the nation won) and adds: this is even more important. Even Lamech, speaking evidently after the fact, thumps his chest in triumph at the revenge he has achieved, surely with an eye to future battles.

Anglo-Saxon poetry, focused mostly on battles, consistently speaks with boasts and taunts, loyalty and honor in the moments of battle. One of many moving battle scenes comes in "The Battle of Maldon" fragment, a poem about the defeat of men of Essex at the hands of invading Vikings in 991. Toward the end of the battle (and the poem,) after some cowards have run away, one old warrior urges his fellows on with words that sound like those of King Henry V and Winston Churchill:

> Courage shall be harder (bolder), heart be keener,
> Mood (spirit) shall be more, as our might lessens.[4]

Even in the face of certain defeat, the cultural values could be celebrated with stirring words. The perspective beyond the present fear is used to build up courage to stand true no matter what the outcome. When a prospective hero is looking for courage to answer the call, the end cannot be known, and the memory of courage can help create courage again.

There was, however, in all this Anglo-Saxon heroic war poetry a sharp distinction made between true and false boasts. In the great epic *Beowulf*, young Beowulf goes to the kingdom of the Danes to help rid their mead hall of the depredations of the monster Grendel. He is welcomed by all but Unferth, who finds Beowulf's venture a "great vexation, because he was not accustomed that any other man in middle-earth ever have more fame" than he himself. Beowulf's reply not only lists his own feats, but calls Unferth "drunk with beer" and suggests his boasts are only like "boy's boasts," not to be carried through. After all, Grendel could never have wreaked such havoc and humiliation, he says to Unferth, "if your courage and your spirit in battle were so fierce in battle as you yourself suppose."[5]

In other words, one's boasts are *good* boasts if one can carry through on them, or, as the current saying goes, it's not bragging if you can do it. The history of one's past and one's lineage, personal and national, is reviewed in a typical Anglo-Saxon boast. It builds courage and evokes loyalty from companions, both qualities highly valued in the warrior worlds of the period. It should also be noted that another possible translation of the word *boast* is "vow," which is perhaps more consonant with modern thinking.

Scriptural and other religious history tales were treated in this same heroic fashion by the Anglo-Saxon world. For example, the poem "The Parting of the Red Sea" has a distinctly heroic and boastful tone in its interpretation of the escape of the Israelites from Egypt. In that account as they approached the water, "a herald stood forth, a valiant leader, uplifting his shield." Then the "people's shepherd" speaks in "words of worth":

> Fear not though Pharaoh may bring against us
> An army of sword-men, a legion of eorls.
> This day our God shall give them reward![6]

In other Anglo-Saxon poetry, the Emperor Constantine's mother, Saint Helena, embarks for the Holy Land to search for the true cross with a "host of eorls" and Saint Andrew leaves Achaia to go "where the Cannibals dwell" in response to God's call, with God himself giving Andrew encouragement by promising to stand by him on his heroic journey.

This kind of warlike interpretation of history can be seen as simply part of the history of a world which saw all of life as a potential war, an attitude that, happily, has now been largely outgrown. We suggest, however, that any movement from the known to the unknown is so difficult that this warlike, taunting attitude is a universal mode of building enough courage to make the move. The task of crossing many human thresholds is so difficult that such litanies of courage and history are needed to help people make that choice. Sometimes it also involves belittling others.

Those who have been involved in wars and battles within living memory will remember, sometimes with embarrassment, the forms of belittling of the other side which were engaged in during the hard times. A recent instance of an attempt to fuel patriotic fervor with mockery appeared in the Argentine press during that country's battle to regain the Falkland Islands. Britain's Prince Andrew, sailing with the Royal Navy, was the brunt of "An Ode to a Baby Corsair," which expressed the hope that the fleet carried disposable diapers "so you won't wet your pants when the fur starts a flyin'."[7] This sort of taunt has a familiar ring to any who have tried to build up courage. It is part of the story of how the threshold can be crossed.

Outside of war, the same practice is engaged in before sporting events, our ritualized heroic battles. Coaches of football, hockey, basketball, and other sports love to find an insulting statement from the other side with which to inspire their troops to higher achievements of revenge. "We'll just see who's a wimp!"

Mohammed Ali is well known for his boastful versifying before a big fight, such as those which began: "Float like a butterfly; sting like a bee." This infuriated some, but seemed to us to be a tongue-in-cheek version of the old boast-vow. It is as if Ali brought in the archetypal trickster to help him.

Such trickster forms of lightening an atmosphere of tension are found in other sports as well. In their drive toward the Super Bowl in 1987, the Denver Broncos, our hometown football team, were apparently beaten in the AFC championship game. Yet a "miracle drive" took the Broncos the length of the field in just about five minutes, winning the right to go on to the Super Bowl. The entire city was charmed by the story of what happened in the huddle in their own end zone as the team faced a seemingly hopeless task. As the team put their heads together, one player, Keith Bishop, is reported to have told his teammates, "Well, guys, we've got them just where we want them!" It was so ludicrous that it evidently relaxed the entire team and allowed them to make a "super" effort.

In the more serious world of real life most cultures develop ritual forms for building up the courage to do what must be done. We saw an enactment of such a ritual in the War Memorial Museum in Auckland, New Zealand, during a special Maori exhibit. In connection with the exhibit, a live program depicting Maori customs was performed. The audience for the program played the part of a visiting party. Three young men dressed as Maori warriors came out armed with spears held threateningly at the ready for attack. Their yells and actions were a ritual show of strength. Then, as the narrator explained to us, a further ritual followed, the essence of which was the discernment of whether the "visiting party" came in friendship or to fight. The interaction between tribes and nations universally develops such rituals, a major part of which is the show of strength and willingness to go to battle if need be. The monomyth pattern suggests that the building up of courage is the other major component.

## Fear of Changing

The terror someone can feel at the threat of trying to change old, even very destructive patterns can be seen from a fragment of a journal written by a woman we will call Peg. She had identified such a destructive pattern in herself and was confronted with the challenge of committing herself to giving it up. That night she woke at 3:00 A.M., struggling with the commitment. She wrote in her journal:

> I go through the possibilities of what would happen if I really let go. I struggle with the idea that I had less than a 50–50 chance of having it all turn out well. Why should it? But I can find no other way. I cannot live the way it is and I don't wish to die this way. I must let go whatever the consequences.
>
> I feel like I'm being asked to walk a tight rope blindfolded although I don't even know how to walk a tight rope without a blindfold. So I would just have to summon the courage—is that the word? No, I have no courage, but if I refuse, I die anyway. I am dammed [*sic*] if I do and dammed [*sic*] if I don't.
>
> Still, I think, I cannot live with myself. I make the decision. I'm exhausted, but the decision is made. I hope I can relax, but I want to strike back! I cry like a baby. I whine. I go out and run. I run and run and stumble. My nose runs. I have no handkerchief. My hands get cold.
>
> Whatever it means—however it is to be done, the commitment is made.

This is an honest example of how awful it can feel to try to go across the threshold, even if a person, like Peg, is truly "dammed" up and "going nowhere" in life if the journey is refused.

Thresholds themselves can be represented by many crossing images—walking a tightrope, crossing rivers, going over bridges or frontiers, or anything which has such a tone of transition. A few examples from dreams will illustrate some of the varied ways in which dreamers are encouraged to go on a journey or are lured forward to the necessary tasks of life.

### Encouragement from a Helper

One such encouragement came by way of a dream to a contemplative monk. Here is his understanding of his dream in his own words:

> I was already a priest a number of years when I entered the monastery at 45. Although I liked the life and the plan very much, I still found adjustment and adaptation very difficult. The silence, the long hours of prayer in common, the night office, the cold, the diet, not to say the amounts of food, all weighed on me. Worse perhaps was the inner turmoil of vivid memories, regrets, longing and the whole bizarre world of confusion and turmoil in the spirit. In the midst of all this stress I had one night a brief dream that had enormous impact, was a profound source of strength to me.
>
> An elderly priest professor of philosophy, austere, devout, dedicated, and long known to me appeared to me bigger than life, looked at me directly, pointed his finger at me and said with emphasis: "What you are doing is a *very beautiful thing*."
>
> That dream nourished me. On the strength of it, I made my vows and entered into this contemplative community and have thanked God ever since for so great a grace.

Telling this dream to a small group, the monk's face lit up. "That dream sustained me," he said. "It made it possible."

There is a numinous quality to the helper who appeared to the monk in his dream; it comes not only from the admiration the monk felt for the professor in outer life, but also in the bigger-than-life appearance and the intensity of the message he brought. In his case the encouragement to go on his lifetime journey of monasticism came from a dream helper. Helpers can appear at any stage of the journey; we discuss them in more detail in Chapter 8.

Notice, though, that even this almost godlike figure still does not make the decision for the dreamer; the helper gives some affirmation and information, but the dreamer chooses what use he will make of it. For this dreamer, the dream was an opening into a fruitful and fulfilled life.

## Fear of Being Alone

The next dream came to a thirty-five-year-old married woman with children. She needed encouragement to go on a second journey right after she had just "returned" from a difficult one:

> I dreamed that I was on an island with a group of people. The leader, who was a man, said that we were all going to swim across the ocean to an island that was visible in the distance. Everyone was enthusiastic. I said that I couldn't make it, that I wasn't strong enough to make it that far. I said that the water was too cold and rough. The man said, "Fine, you stay here by yourself." Everyone started their journey, and I went along so I wouldn't be left alone. I reached the island with ease and had really enjoyed the water. It was warm and calm. There was a beautiful palace on the island. I entered the palace and was awed by its beauty.

Though the dream seems happy, it came at a very difficult time in her life. She had finally called a halt to some thoughtless emotional battering which her mother had practiced against her for years. She had never thought she would be able to do this, and she felt a sense of achievement.

Just as this task was accomplished, though, as so often seems to happen on the hero journey, she was faced with another, even harder, one: to her shock her husband suddenly announced he might want to leave their marriage. She had just found the strength to stand up to her mother, but she felt powerless and helpless before this new threat—and very alone.

This compensatory dream picks up the sense of being left alone, but here no helper appears. She is told casually that she can stay there if she wishes, but the rest are moving on. Yet the dream says that once she takes the plunge (even if only from fear) she can deal with the ocean with ease. It is warm and calm, and she is then rewarded by a strong image of beauty and wholeness—what Jung called a Self image—in the island palace.

At the time she felt abandoned and weak and could feel none of the promise in the dream. The encouragement she needed to move ahead in her life came only from the dream itself. The images in the dream hold out a good prognosis for her ability to deal with whatever is called for in the journey and for the wholeness which can be hers when she stays with her journey, and this in itself helped give her the energy she needed. It may even be that the fear of being alone and feeling herself inadequate to life's tasks without others to depend on was itself the task. If so, the dream showed that her central fear could be used to urge her onward.

## Wounded Confidence

The next dreamer is a minister who had been an assistant and then the minister in charge on an interim basis of a large urban congregation. He felt he was doing an excellent job, and his confidence was at a high level. Then the search committee told him that his name had been removed from the list of candidates for their church. This was a blow to his pride and created a strong feeling of uncertainty for his future. Furthermore, he was very angry at the congregation—people he had loved and helped through difficult times.

At this point he had a dream which encouraged him:

> I was in my office standing in front of a desk. I looked down and saw metal cages with different kinds of birds in each cage. I looked on top of the desk and there were cages of birds, one in each cage, lying on their sides with their feet sticking out. I didn't like all those birds in my office and it gave me a creepy feeling. I spotted one, hanging by its feet, upside down directly above me. None of these birds were moving.
> 
> My brother, who is a physician, appeared and told me all of these birds were sick or wounded, but they were all going to get well. He took a few of them to the window and they sprang to life and flew away. I knew they were all alive, but they were certainly wounded or sick.
> 
> I noticed a squirrel in one of the cages. The fur was missing from the back half of its body. I asked my brother about it and he said that it would be healed too.
> 
> Then I was in the parish hall of a church talking with a recognizable priest. He told me he had cancer. He and his wife began shrinking away, getting shorter and smaller. I turned to the congregation with a warm feeling in my heart and ministered to all of them. I felt very

good. I also knew the priest didn't really have cancer. He was decreasing and I was increasing. The people were grieving, but we were all together in our grief, and it was okay.

As he worked on the dream, it seemed to have three successive images of being hurt and trapped and then being freed. The birds evoked for him the sense of his own spirit, wounded by the congregation's rejection, which had cut very deep. The squirrel, a little animal he liked to watch move fast through the trees, had lost "the hide off his back"—again, how he himself felt.

His own resentment was like a cancer growing in him, but in all three of these images, there was healing or freeing promised. His brother came to him as a healing physician to assure him his wounded instincts would recover. He could get out of the cage of his own pain.

The dream also makes clear, though, that he and the people can experience their grief and be together in that. The last scene in the dream helped give him the energy to feel his genuine regard and love—which in turn freed him to minister, even in his grief. The dream does not specify more than this what his journey will be about or how he will come home again, but it does give him the courage to go into the darkness. Perhaps his journey, despite the lack of confidence he felt, is really the classical journey from hubris to humility, but coming via the dream with the message that humility is not the end of his world. He will become someone better by taking his dark journey.

### Bringing Bolivia Home

A consoling dream came to a former missionary two years after her return to the United States after more than eighteen years in Bolivia. Though she tried to enjoy her work in the United States, she seemed to continue mourning, as over a death—as she put it, "Mine to Bolivia and Bolivia's to me." The dream came when she had just begun to sense some resonance to her life again:

> I looked up and saw Pedro standing there. He was crying floods of tears. I approached him to console him and suddenly noticed he was not crying. Instead, he said to me, "Don't be so sad, come and see

José's new car." So we took each other by the hand and walked until we turned a corner. There was José standing with a big smile and next to him a small white car with the hatchback open.

Before this dream she had had a number of other car dreams, always with the jeep she drove in Bolivia, and always with the car in awkward places, such as inside a swimming pool. This dream was a relief, as there was a new car, in an appropriate place, and everyone greeted her and the car with smiles and encouragement.

The people in the dream were two friends from Bolivia. Pedro was a little boy whose birth she saw, the son of a family she lived with. He was her godchild and she loved him very much. This small animus figure was inviting her to stop her sadness and move toward a new way of getting around—a new car.

José was another friend, "a very generous young man." He was a cultural promoter to the Aymara people she so admired and, she added, "maybe a helper and male animus figure for me." When her friends came to her in this light, positive dream, she was able to see the possibilities in her new life, instead of just feeling alone and afraid.

It is interesting that in the years following this dream, her new work blossomed, and she herself was able to start creative new programs for the poor and disadvantaged. Her new journey involved the vision to see what was needed back in her home country and bring the skills and insight from her foreign missionary work back home. By seeing what was needed back in the United States, she too became a "cultural promoter" of people. The friends in her dream helped her cross over into a new life. Though they lived so far from her now, through their appearance in her dream they helped incorporate her into her new journey in her new community by their encouragement.

### The Neanderthal Men

An amusing (and amazing) dream came to a very proper and traditional woman whose children were grown and married. At the time of the dream she was going through a period of depression and reexamination of her life and attitudes. In the course of this work she decided that throughout her life she had failed to *live* as fully as she could have. This awareness filled her with a sense of despair and anger, followed by the determination to try to do something about it, even at this late date. Despite her determination, she continued to fight against the inner negative thought that it was "too late" to change.

For example, she saw that she had always said what she thought she was expected to say. In response to that insight, she made some efforts to assert what she really thought about events, instead of just saying what she thought people expected to hear. About that time she had this dream:

> My husband and I were watching the procession into church. In the procession were two naked neanderthal men, rather short and stocky, with short legs and very hairy, with black hair almost like black turf. I saw them only from the back, but I knew they had no clothes in front either. (I thought: maybe they're so hairy nothing will "show.") I thought this was very inappropriate for church, even if historically correct. I said to my husband that only our minister would have dared include them.

The minister in the dream was actually her minister, a man she respected highly, especially for his courage in bringing *reality* instead of just traditional teaching into a rather proper church.

These two naked neanderthal men probably represented her efforts to bring more reality into her own interactions with other people. She feared her new ways were out of place in church. Perhaps her own efforts to develop and exercise her "masculine" side were at a primitive level. She was probably also feeling that her own assertiveness might "show" too much, as the dream humorously suggests in her fears about the inappropriateness of the naked men in church. She had answered the call to adventure by making some changes, but the crossing was troubling to her.

Yet at the same time, despite her own doubts, she also admired the spiritual leader who dared bring the men there—a strong encouragement to her to take the risk of being more real. Her dream places the naked men right in the church procession.

We could go on endlessly relating dreams which demonstrate the variety of ways in which dreamers are helped to get the courage to cross the threshold. The potential hero is helped across the threshold by anger, rage, determination, patriotic fervor, loyalty, humor, helpers, even resignation.

As will be noted from these examples, the form in which encouragement comes frequently seems to fit precisely with the dreamer. It is almost as if the dream-maker says, in effect, "You're afraid of being alone? I'll show you what alone can be like." Or maybe, "You're not sure it is right for you to be a monk? Who would impress you? That's who will come in your dream!"

# ▶8

# Discernment: Helpers or Tempters

Either at the time one is attempting to gain enough courage to cross the threshold or at other points on the journey, with all its tests and trials, one encounters the problem of descernment, for there are both helpers and tempters along the way. The problem is: which is which?

Judas, the disciple who betrayed Jesus, failed not only in discernment, but also in accepting the humiliation of his mistake. We do not know the motivation for his betrayal. Thirty pieces of silver does not seem enough for a disciple who has responded to Jesus' call and who has walked the path of his ministry throughout Galilee and Judea. Down through the centuries Christians have speculated on this.

One suggestion we find appealing is that he really believed Jesus was the Messiah, but he did not understand what Jesus said about the meaning of "Messiah." One of the popular ideas in Jesus' day was that the Messiah, whom God would send to free his people from foreign oppression, would lead armies against the enemy—either earthly armies or heavenly, angelic armies. Perhaps Judas was trying to force Jesus' hand, to make him reveal his power by calling down heavenly hosts. Perhaps he thought he could use the high priests as helpers, did not recognize them as tempters.

Certainly Judas was not satisfied with the money alone, for when he saw Jesus would not start a rebellion, but would submit to crucifixion instead, in his despair he flung the money back and hung himself. In the end one could say he lacked the courage to face his mistake in discernment. He was not open to other possibilities. He did not have, as Jesus said, "ears to hear." Perhaps he was not listening when Jesus told the story of a wayward son whose father, without needing to hear his apology, rushed down the road to meet him and welcome him with a feast.

In fairy tales a common helper is the *friendly animal* who comes to the aid of one who is open to receive such unusual aid, or a "good fairy," as in Cinderella. It was a "good witch" that came to Dorothy's aid in *The Wizard of Oz*.

Helpers may have an ugly appearance when first encountered, or as fairy tales often put it, they may be "loathsome." Tempters, on the other hand, may look very good, only to trap the unwary; but sometimes, to win through to the treasure, heads must be chopped off. Tempters may urge one not to move forward, not to complete some task; they may tempt one to keep the status quo even after one has undertaken a few initial steps on the journey.

In fairy tales it is witches who cast the binding spells. In life it may even be one's parents who do this, without conscious intention. They may simply be concerned with protection and want to keep their child at home—not venturing out. Unconsciously, parents may also want their child to live out the parents' vision rather than the child's.

One image of a parent thus limiting a child is depicted as the relation between a falconress and the hooded falcon on her wrist by the poet Robert Duncan in "My Mother Would Be a Falconress":

My mother would be a falconress,
And I, her gay falcon treading her wrist,
would fly to bring back from the blue sky to her, bleeding, a prize,
where I dream in my little hood with many bells
jangling when I'd turn my head.[1]

The speaker's "dreaming" in his "little hood" gives the reader a sense of his being too controlled by his mother, of his not being able to grow up and become his own person, because she continues to limit him and he to accept the limitation. The falcon, after all, *could* fly away when loosed from the wrist, but his taming and training make him return to captivity with his bleeding prize. The poem continues with descriptive images of the limitation of not being free from the mother, who only "sends me as far as her will goes"—and no farther. This is a kind of enmeshment and attempt to control the child which many dysfunctional families experience.

This kind of paralysis is also pictured by John Keats in "La Belle Dame Sans Merci"; his beautiful lady is truly without pity on the narrator. He is a knight who is asked at the beginning of the poem what ails him "alone and palely loitering." He describes meeting the beautiful lady and taking her on his horse with him to an elfin grotto where she lulled him to sleep. Sleeping, he dreamed:

> I saw pale kings and princes too,
>   Pale warriors, death-pale were they all;
> They cried—"La Belle Dame sans merci
>   Hath thee in thrall?"[2]

This knight is the antithesis of the faithful quester, and his bewitchment dooms him to paralyzed inactivity. In psychological language, such entrapment represents the temptation to regression, infancy, helplessness, or unconsciousness—the most dangerous aspect of the hero journey.

A common motif in fairy tales is: that which looks ugly in the beginning is often beautiful when one goes through the experience, or has a gentle spirit that is open to learning. Often in fairy tales it is the *youngest* son or daughter who has the gentle spirit. The youngest goes on the journey less sure of already knowing everything—ready to learn and able to receive help. In fact, the relation to the helpful animal in fairy tales guarantees the success of the venture. Marie-Louise von Franz says, "In all the myths and fairytales I have studied, I have never seen a case where a hero with helpful animals does not win out. If he picks up a helpful or a grateful animal who had promised to help, with absolute certainty it can be predicted that there will not be a tragedy but a happy end."[3] A typical story has three sons admonished by their father to accomplish some task. The eldest ventures out, only to find he must embrace some loathsome hag; he returns emptyhanded. The second son also finds the hag too disgusting. The third son ventures forth, accepts the challenge of embracing the hag, and wins the prize. The loathsome old woman turns out to be a beautiful princess who has been under a spell.

What do such fairy tales suggest? Like any true symbol, they suggest many things, no one of which is the whole story. One could say: courage to undertake the distasteful, a certain innocence or gentleness of spirit (the "youngest" daughter or son), an openness to things not being as they seem, and a willingness to take the risk. Being willing to discover or learn a new perspective is essential; also, and perhaps more important, to remain true to one's call, to maintain one's integrity. In Shakespeare's *King Lear* it is Cordelia, the youngest of the king's three daughters, who has the courage to resist greed and not compromise her integrity.

In the film *Chariots of Fire* both of the principal characters face temptations. Harold, when defeated by Eric the first time, wants to give up; his fiancée tries to talk him out of it in the stadium scene, but he is able to choose to go on only when a new coach agrees to help him learn how to win. Beaten once, he does not want to go on. Later, he faces a still different temptation, when two college elders, presenting themselves as "helpers," have him to dinner and tell him he should practice like a "gentleman" without the professional coach. They want him to follow college "customs," which, they hint, will make him "acceptable." As a Jew, the film makes clear, he still will not be "acceptable" to them. Harold must make his choice: is his coach or are the college elders the true tempters, enticing him from his heroic path?

Eric, the Scotsman, finds a tempter in his sister, who urges him not to compete as a runner. He will be, she tells him, abandoning God's call. He resists, however, and tells her it is God who, after all, is the one who made him "fast." Then, when a race is set on Sunday, which he believes to be the day which must be set apart for worship, the opposite kind of temptation is presented. The Prince of Wales tells him it is his duty to run. Temptations from every angle! Discernment is not easy, but it is part of the task of the hero journey.

A similar problem arises in dreams with reference to various shadow figures and anima or animus figures. Are they tempters or helpers, good guys or bad guys? The dreams themselves can help one discern which choice in outer life one wishes to make by the very clarity with which the dream image presents the help.

### The Angel Sponsor

This dream was clearly a dream of a helper, and the angelic helper helped the dreamer discern where she wanted to go in her life and how to get there. She wrote us a letter which speaks of her helper, and we quote from it at length:

"I'll tell you a little about myself, then give you my dream and finally share the interpretation you helped me with. It might be helpful to know that this dream interpretation has helped me many times since then to know where I am and to remind myself that I must stick to my discipline and not give in to bitterness, fatigue or discouragement.

"I am a 40-year-old woman. I have a deep spiritual life which I consider to be more important than anything else in my life. I was raised a Roman Catholic and now am a member of a Baptist church in my home town. I belong to a lay, contemplative religious order in the Episcopal Church. My spirituality would be characterized more Catholic and Episcopal than what is commonly considered Baptist. I am more contemplative than action oriented. I meditate daily and have learned how to know what God is telling me in my dreams. I use imaging all the time. I have had visions in the last year, beginning with one at the moment my mother died at her home 40 miles south of my home.

"I write fiction full time. I quit or 'retired from' my career as a journalist and in public relations three years ago to write fiction full time. Although I have had many nonfiction pieces published, my fiction has not been published yet.

"I have been married for 15 years to a university professor, writer, counselor.

"When I entered puberty I became overweight. My weight and food in general became an obsession with me. I tried bulimia in college. Then when my husband told me in no uncertain terms before we were married that he would not have a fat wife I became seriously bulimic. It was the only way I could keep from getting fat. I was moderately overweight at the time, mostly from frequent crash diets. I was bulimic for 13 years. A year and a half ago, I realized I was killing myself. I couldn't stop however and finally told God: this is hopeless. Help me. He led me, literally moments after that prayer, to Overeaters Anonymous, a twelve-step program based on the twelve steps of Alcoholics Anonymous. From the day I joined OA, I have not been bulimic and have not gained an ounce. My entire life has changed. I'm learning to feel my feelings. It turns out that what I usually feel is fear. I'm learning not to deny and stuff those feelings but to learn healthy behaviors. I don't isolate anymore. I call people in the program. Until recently I've had a sponsor, and I'm looking for another one now. This is someone you call every day and when you are having a problem. You talk instead of eat. I'm learning to live one day at a time. More than anything, I'm learning to give up trying to control others or my environment. I have since joined Al-Anon (for families and friends of alcoholics) and Adult Children of Alcoholics (ACA). Both my parents were alcoholic. I was physically, emotionally, and sexually abused as a child. I'm learning not to deny that these things happened and that they hurt me today. I'm learning (slowly) that there are people I *can* trust and that I will never be abandoned again—because I won't abandon me. I can parent myself. I can reach out to other people in the program, too.

"It's important to realize in interpreting this dream that to successfully work the program I must constantly follow the steps and avoid the pitfalls. There are things I can't eat and times I can't eat. There are many times I quit eating when I am frantic to binge. I must feel feelings when it seems easier to deny them and eat or isolate. I must *work* the steps. To relax or give in is literally death for me because I will be bulimic again before I will ever allow myself to be fat.

"This is the dream:

> Someone, like a constant sponsor or guardian angel, female, was telling me how well I had done. "You made your mother go into there (the water?) with your aunt." She was consoling me that I was better than I thought. When she said that, I had this image of my mother and my aunt walking ahead of me and I saw that the force of my "Being" caused them to go into this pool together, someplace they would never have gone of their own free will.
> 
> Someone accused me of overeating, getting fat. I said I had not and I looked to this angel for support. She backed me up. I was handing something to her and just went ahead and scraped some of the frosting off in my mouth, even though she saw me and I wasn't supposed to. Then I was going on, preparing to prepare a meal, bitterly realizing that although I had been on my new eating discipline for some time and had lost weight that I would have to be on it for a long, long time to come and there was nothing I could do about it.

Not only that, but I was being given a baby to take care of. As I gathered up diapers and things, I was bitter and resigned to the burden and drudgery of this responsibility in addition to the already grinding responsibility of the eating discipline. The angel was there throughout. The baby was a baby, but had been a baby for a long, long time.

"*Message:* The second part of the dream folds back on the first. At one level, the first part of the dream in itself is an affirmation that I did the right thing in learning to be myself and persevering in that when my mother was dying. She and my father wanted me to continue to live the lie that I was bad, the cause of everything bad in their lives and unloveable. But I didn't. My mother and my aunt in me died because I became strong enough to exist.

"There is a strong, constant presence that encourages and comforts me, defends me against accusers and does not punish me when I fail. This presence is God and is the spirit of strength, persistance and courage within me. A shadow figure—a self figure that has the ability to carry me through. It is my ability to parent myself.

"The second part of the dream is a warning not to let bitterness and tiredness turn me away from the discipline and orderliness (opposite of dis-order, as in eating disorder) that I need. Bitterness or giving up the orderliness and discipline will lead to my disappearance into the pool of unconsciousness like my mother and my aunt. They both lived lives of denial and lies, and I did too until I learned the discipline of the 12-step program. Denial is fatal, literally, for bulimics just as it is for alcoholics.

"The baby is my writing. The writing is an additional burden of responsibility that requires tremendous discipline. It all *is* very exhausting. A counselor also told me to go ahead and *be* angry and not to turn it in. The healing power of the constant presence, the self figure or shadow, is bringing me the bitterness for my healing."

After working through this dream, she found that she was, in the months which followed, much better able to "feel some things," commenting a year later that she did not think she's ever allowed herself "to feel" in her life before her heroic changes. She even found herself able to write with more ease and peace.

Like most hero journeys, hers was difficult and lengthy, but the helper "angel sponsor" gave her the courage to believe in her ability to make it. "The angel was there throughout."

### The Big Black Dog

The next dream has a true "friendly animal," who helps the dreamer through a stormy journey. The first scene of the dream, or "encounter," as the dreamer called it, reminds us of an episode in a Narnia tale, *The Horse and His Boy*. In a scene toward the end of that novel the young hero, Shasta, must travel through a mountain pass at night, while the other characters he has been traveling with are allowed to rest. He is feeling sorry for himself and put upon, when he suddenly finds himself accompanied by an unseen companion. The companion listens to his complaints through the night and, he later discovers, had carefully walked between Shasta and the edge of a precipice he could not see in the dark. The companion was, of course, the Christ figure of Narnia, the lion Aslan.[4]

The following dreamer had a similar helper in her "first encounter":

> In my dream I had three encounters.
>
> I was in a storm and lost, but a large black dog stayed by my side to protect and guide me. At times, he seemed much larger than I was. He was on my left side as we walked through the snow. But when I would turn right, there he was on my right side, nudging me back to the path. Whichever way I would turn, he would be on that side, preventing me from veering off the path.
>
> Then I was inside a room, talked with Jim. He was in one of his "fatherly" moods. I was tempted to play up to him—to be a little girl. But I didn't. We just talked as adults about my present state in life.
>
> The third encounter—I cannot remember. My therapist was there. She appeared, but either I walked away or she receded.

This was the dream of a middle-aged woman who entered therapy to work on a complex of personal devaluation and helplessness. She felt helpless to say what she really thought to people or even to think she had any right to do so. For example, the man Jim, who appears in her second "encounter," was her boss in a former job, and she had never been able to confront him about his treatment of her, no matter how inappropriate it was. She left that job rather than tell him that she wanted to be treated as an adult. This dream scene is therefore contrary to fact in her past experience.

The dream thus seems to be pointing her toward some new behavior which may be possible for her, even though it has not yet come to pass. The dog, her protector and guide in the first scene, provides the clue that there is some inner help available for her, even though it may only be at a very instinctual level as yet. In thinking about the dream, she remembered that she had once been frightened by a large black dog as a little girl, so the image was scary for her. The dog was scary, yet it was her helper and protector. This is like many of the fairy tale characters who frighten the heroes, but who are really there to help them complete their journeys.

Reporting the dream to her therapist, she felt a lot of emotion when she discussed the third encounter, hazy as it was. As they worked through the first two scenes, the helper in the first and the power she felt in remaining an adult in the second enabled her to confront the therapist with an issue which had long bothered her in their work. The whole of the dream thus signaled a turnaround for her in her ability to confront life situations straightforwardly, without veering from the path or regressing into childish behavior. The dream itself seemed to carry the energy for her to begin to make a courageous change.

## Befriending the Bull

A discernment process was reflected and affirmed by a brief dream which came to a woman in her mid-thirties while she was pregnant with her first child. She was excited about the pregnancy, but found herself continually swept with fears—of infection or harm to the baby she carried. About this same time the town where she lived was the site of a fatal commercial airplane crash. Fear again gripped her, because she and her husband were in the midst of planning a long airplane trip to visit her family.

One night she lay awake grappling with her fears until she just "acknowledged" them. In effect, she stopped trying not to be afraid and simply admitted that she was. Then what? What was there to do about it—never travel by airplane again? That would be like not having a baby because something might go wrong. She then spoke to herself about what she did believe in: a God who was an underlying, benevolent wisdom in the universe who takes care of us. There was no guarantee in the world, but she was able to relax into this caring wisdom. Subsequently, she had this dream:

> A bull was chasing me. I saw a way of escape over a wall. I had to go straight for it. There was no time to look back and assess the situation. I got onto the top of the wall. Then I decided to ride on the back of the bull and use it as my *ally*.

She knew that the bull represented her fear which continually "chased" her, and she felt that riding the bull in the dream was an image of acknowledging her fear and dealing with it. To add to this confirmation, her next dream in the same night was one of being with all her family in a loving, warm, accepting atmosphere. These two dreams were for her a real affirmation of the choice she made in the night. The bull was like the power she could now ride as she joyfully embraced life with all its risks.

### The Wolf and the Camel

The following remarkable dream came to a thirty-five-year-old man, a psychotherapist, whom we will call Phil. At the time of the dream Phil had been hurt badly by a crisis in his outer life, which threatened his professional life and his family. He knew on waking that the dream was very important, but it unfolded itself only gradually to him:

> I don't know what I was, but my father was a one-humped camel, a great, large, famous one, and my mother was a great silver wolf. I became lost in the deep snow and was once caught by some large animals, but escaped down into a cave. I think I was wounded, hurt, but fell into a den of wolves, and the mother took me in. I fell down, down, down inside and from the outside you could not even find the opening. I can vaguely remember someone (the mother) going around kicking off the snow so that light would go down inside the den.
> Next I (whatever I was) was in a race (car race) down a long hill, very steep and narrow. All these other cars were racing and at the very end and when the race was almost over, I took my turn. I went to get in the starting gate, similar to a ski racers gate, and there was another

car there. People were laughing, saying my car would never win—it was so strange. I finally got in the gate and won the race and said that my father was the great one-humped camel and my mother was the great silver wolf.

His personal associations with the two "parents" in the dream were positive. The silver wolf reminded him of a character in a children's book, *Barrington Bunny,* in which a wolf faithfully stands sentinel over his friend's body when he dies. He also associated the wolf with a movie he loved, *Never Cry Wolf,* that had beautiful scenery and portrayed wolves as loving, strong, caring. Though "den of wolves" normally has a negative connotation, the image was positive for him. A den of wolves was—to him—a supportive community.

The camel likewise had a positive association for Phil from another children's book, by Madeleine L'Engle, about a boy who goes to the Sphinx. The boy was protected by a camel, who, as well as the dreamer could remember, gave the boy the answers to the Sphinx's questions.

The cars in the second part of the dream, he said, were like those in a soapbox derby—made by the drivers.

On waking, he knew that the most crucial action in the dream was making sure that the light could get into the cave. The mother wolf was the one who kicked the snow away so the light could come in. At that point, he could not connect the dream with his life, but it was so strange and so numinous that he could not forget it either. Through the months that followed, he simply carried the memory of the dream around with him in the back of his mind, knowing that the most crucial thing was for the light to come in.

Readers of the dream and of his associations can see several motifs which give clues to its meaning. He is lost in deep snow, which is certainly how he felt in the crisis he was in. It is also clear that he is unsure of himself, perhaps has a weak ego, does not know "who he is." It is also clear that he *does* win the race in the end, despite the mocking laughter of the bystanders. His wounding and healing in the cave are also clear, but why the animal parents, and why does he refer to them again after he wins the race? It almost sounds as if he is able to win in part because of these animal parents.

From the standpoint of the monomyth of the hero, the dream can be identified as belonging to the lower part of the circle, the road of trials and tasks. The animal parents are helpers. The cave appears to be part of a dark retreat, such as the hero's movement into the lower darkness of the journey. This cave seems to connect him with the depths of the earth itself for the healing—much as wounded animals go to earth to be nursed back to health while they lie in a protected place.

After several years of work on his outer and inner life, greater understanding of the dream "clicked" for him. Throughout these years, as we said, Phil had held the memory of the dream close. Such a dream can nurture and energize a dreamer, even without understanding it.

As a child, he had felt inferior, both to his austere, authoritarian, dry (and somewhat famous) father and to his high-achieving siblings. Even his mother, though positive for him in some ways, supported his father's austerity by her passivity. No one in the family ever gave him affirmation for his very deep and real feeling gifts—the very gifts that enabled him to do good work in his helping profession. So, of course, since no one valued him for these gifts, he himself did not appreciate them—his feelings were frozen, lost as in deep snow.

The dream puts him in touch with repressed instinctual values of undifferentiated but powerful, archetypal nurturing and healing parental forces. He is wounded, but with time, when the light comes in, he can be healed and win his race—in part *because* of these mysterious, instinctual "parents." The dream imagery gave him, in a sense, archetypal parents who were supportive and affirming in place of the lack of support he had felt growing up. The cave, in the earth, is like going back to nature and letting the supporting part of nature and the community of wolves serve him for healing, as the wolves nursed the legendary founders of Rome. After that happens, the dream promises that he can win the race.

It may even prove true for Phil, as it has for many, that such powerful animal dream figures remain important throughout one's entire life. They thus become a kind of individuating or particularizing totem for the dreamer, continuing to carry a sense of meaning and significance, which gradually unfolds itself into personal awareness. If so, the camel and wolf may be seen as tutelary spirits whose traits have a specific qualitative relational significance to Phil's personal development. In many stories, a weakness in the hero "who is endeavoring to discover and assert his personality" is balanced by the appearance of strong tutelary or guardian figures who are symbolic representatives of the whole psyche.[5] They supply the strength the personal ego lacks.

This is analogous to contemporary anthropological theories of the meaning of the practice of totemism.[6] When totemism is practiced, such totem figures can become carriers and markers of identity and meaning, in much the way that the totem animal of a dream vision carried identity and meaning to initiated youth in an earlier time.

In what Jung might call a synchronicity, we found out through a telephone call that Phil had had another wolf dream—just as this book was going to press and after the above interpretation had been written. Here is the second wolf dream:

> I was doing group therapy with another therapist with three couples, but the office was out of doors in an opening in the forest. I was talking with one of the women as she sat near the trees about what good work she had done in therapy. I told her she had done such good work that there was no need for her to go on with therapy. I also told her that I had done very good work, too, in helping her to do her work.
>
> Just then two enormous golden wolves appeared over her shoulder as we talked—almost like sentinels. I knew instantly who they were. I told the woman, "If I hadn't done my job, those wolves would have something to say about it."
>
> Then I asked the wolves what they wanted from me. They began laughing and dancing and playing and jumping on each other like dogs might do. They gave me no verbal answer, but that was all the answer I needed!
>
> Then the scene switched back to the office, and I began to move furniture around to get ready for the group, feeling frustrated with the other therapist for not taking initiative.

Phil said that he woke the next morning after the dream and went downstairs to make some coffee. As he began to climb the stairs with the coffee, he suddenly remembered the dream. As he did, tears began streaming down his face. He said the feeling he had on remembering the dancing wolves was of security, comfort, and passion—just "incredible security."

The context of the dream in his life situation was an argument with his wife. Earlier such an argument would have left him feeling shattered and insecure, but after this one he realized that he had attained a strong sense of inner security—he knew he could "make it" no matter what happened in outer life. The dream followed that realization and seems a strong confirmation of his newfound sense of security.

The dream also places this security in the context of Phil's professional work, suggesting that he is able to do "good work" as a therapist because he has done his own inner work. As he claims this ability, his "totem" wolves appear, frolicking in joy. They are a pair, suggesting an integration of some of his inner conflicts. They are also golden, as opposed to the silver wolf in his first dream, and gold is traditionally associated with masculine, as silver is with feminine. Perhaps these two wolves are also confirming that his way of being masculine, though different from the stereotypes, is appropriate for him. There may also be a suggestion that he is more differentiated from the nurturing mother wolf in the first dream, perhaps through relating to the woman anima over whose shoulder the wolves appear. This may be the meaning of the "good work" the anima figure had done, so that now she does not need any more therapy.

There is a warning implicit in the dream as well, both in the recognition that the "wolves would have something to say" if he did not do his own work and also in the other (shadow?) therapist, who does not "take initiative." Phil needs to continue to stay very conscious and keep up his "good work," or else he may have "wolves nipping at his heels," as he put it.

Phil had recently moved into a new office at the time of this last dream, and he had unearthed a wood block print made for him fourteen years before by someone he had helped. The wood print portrayed the great silver wolf from *Barrington Bunny*. Phil decided he would frame it and hang it in his new office as a reminder of his strong tutelary helpers.

Let us repeat that helpers and tempters can appear at every stage of the journey; many examples are offered in other sections of this book. The discernment of their appropriate role is, in one sense, part of the task of the hero. The hero is one who can recognize and accept help, resist the tempters, and incorporate the wisdom of the helpers into his or her own individuation process.

# ▶9
## The Road of Trials

Once having crossed the threshold of adventure, responded to the call, and endured the pain of separation, the hero is faced with a series of trials, or a succession of tasks to be accomplished. In the fairy tales and stories from different cultures the tasks and trials are frequently portrayed as physical obstacles or undertakings. As we have said, however, the road of trials in the hero journey is also about the interior experience of the individual, a matter of inner growth and development. The symbolic meaning of those episodes in the hero's journey is the process by which the hero becomes someone more than she or he was before the journey.

In *The Uses of Enchantment* Bruno Bettelheim defends the reading of fairy tales. He says that life is a struggle for meaning and that the struggle is lifelong.[1] Crises emerge in childhood as well as in adult life, although, he argues, parents do not often recognize this. Fairy tales symbolically represent the problems in development, and they include portrayals of the tasks and trials as well as the victories in overcoming them. Parents, Bettelheim thinks, too often oppose the fairy tales precisely because they have this dark aspect, and thus existential problems get ignored. Fairy tales, while portraying the problems of life, set them at a distance, a step removed. Also, fairy tales show the triumphs over obstacles and so give hope to the child for the conflicts presently being experienced.

Through fantasy and portrayals in story, the individual—child or adult—is helped to come to terms with something. This is not solely a conscious or intentional process, but a process natural to the psyche. Sleep laboratories that have studied the effects of dreaming tell us much the same thing—that dreaming is a necessary function for one's mental and physical health, regardless of the fact that the dream may not even be remembered, let alone understood symbolically. Psychological concepts are not necessary; however, working with one's dreams and trying to understand their symbolic language, we feel, helps one to enter the process consciously and use that additional data in making the decisions that need to be made.

Images in this lower half of the circle tend to be frightening, dangerous, and desolate. As Jung puts it, "The purpose of the descent as universally exemplified in the myth of the hero is to show that only in the region of danger (watery abyss, cavern, forest, island, castle, etc.) can one find the 'treasure hard to attain' (jewel, virgin, life-potion, victory over death)."[2] Sometimes the road of trials is generically described in the stories as a "night sea journey" or as the experience in the "belly of the whale." The biblical story of Jonah, of course, uses this latter image. Jonah was told by God to go preach to the city of Ninevah, but instead Jonah tried to flee from that call and took ship. When a terrible storm arose, the people on board sought to determine who was responsible and, after casting lots, determined that it was Jonah. They cast him into the sea, but a huge fish swallowed Jonah and after three days spit him up on shore in the direction he was to go. The call can be insistent.

Many Bible commentators have suggested that the baptism of Jesus was his "call," as well as the acceptance of his mission. Immediately afterward, he experienced a separation, a kind of threshold crossed, for he was led by the Spirit into the wilderness to fast. Then he was tempted by the Devil—a demanding "trial of strength."

The task of the hero journey requires one to learn and experience not only one's strengths and abilities, but also to learn one's weaknesses. The journey often entails the turning of what at first seemed to be an obstacle into an aid. When confronted, what appeared to be a dangerous monster or dragon may become the steed that bears one swiftly forward on the journey. In Jungian terminology this might be referred to as confrontation with and assimilation of the shadow.

Jung tells one such dream of his own: it begins with Jung and an "unknown, brown-skinned man, a savage, in a lonely, rocky mountain landscape." Jung and the savage then killed Siegfried, after which Jung was filled with disgust and remorse "for having destroyed something so great and beautiful." Jung offers little interpretation of the dream except to say that the savage was "an embodiment of the primitive shadow," and to say that energy was released in him to carry on his experiment with the unconscious.[3]

The dream came in 1913, after Jung's break with Freud as he searched for his own "footing." Anthony Storr, commenting on the Siegfried dream, points out that such dreams of the sacrifice of the hero are typical of dreams occurring in middle life when a change of attitude is demanded. He connects the dream to the sacrifice Jung made at the time, giving up his position as a teacher at the University of Zurich, which Jung himself had described as a great risk, one he took in order to focus on his work with the unconscious.[4]

In Jung's understanding of the developmental process, which he called the "individuation process," one has to come to terms with the "other side," the unconscious part of one's psyche. This includes not only the shadow, but also, for a man, a feminine aspect which he most likely projects on a woman; and for a woman, a masculine aspect which is usually projected on a man. Unless this more mysterious, more unconscious aspect of oneself (represented by an opposite-sex figure) has been integrated and brought into some awareness or consciousness, one is subject to "seeing" those traits and characteristics in another person and feeling either attracted or repelled by them. This unconscious mechanism is known in psychology as a "projection." It is not something people consciously do or have; rather, the projections "have" them. The journey of spiritual growth entails some coming to terms with this aspect of oneself. The hero stories often portray these as outward encounters, and they also appear as such in people's dreams.

The road of trials gets one outside of oneself. Thus, anyone, in whatever society, who undertakes the perilous journey into the unknown, into the darkness, is descending into the lanes and byways of his or her inmost being. It will probably manifest itself as a maze, a labyrinth, something through which one must find one's way. The maze at Chartres Cathedral, for example, is understood as a symbolic representation of the spiritual journey of life.

In the language of the mystical tradition in Christianity, the road of trials is "the way of purification." The purgation stage of the mystical path is one in which the senses are "cleansed and humbled," and the energies are concentrated on transcendental things.

The ultimate task of the hero stories, which describe the tasks of life, is for the hero to come into relationship with a larger meaning than the development of the ego. The tasks involve the connection of the ego (as fully as it has developed) with the Self, the archetype of wholeness. The task of the first half of life is inappropriate when carried over into the afternoon of life, though if the tasks of the first half are incomplete (no matter what the age), aspects of "first half" journeys may appear in older people. Yet the ultimate goal of the adult hero journey is to find, win, achieve, a sense of meaning and confidence—a new perspective on one's place in the universe.

### Cleaning Up the Mess

This great middle part of the journey, as we have said, includes the tasks to be achieved, frequently with some kind of sacrificial action, always with tests to be passed. This dream of a thirty-seven-year-old married professional woman is especially interesting because of its extravagant language and mundane subject matter. What the psyche labels as heroic may not seem so at first glance.

The dream occurred not long after her father's death:

> Several members of my family are together—my mother, my father, my oldest sister and me.
> My parents are old, but instead of being at their nursing home, we are all on a ship.
> My father calls out from the bathroom. He has urinated and defecated all over the floor, and cleaning it up is my job. It's nauseating, but somehow I don't mind too much—it's sort of a part of life.
> Then I am outside, in a rural area, about to make a telephone call to my husband. I have grey hair, but I feel—more than look—very young. I think about how glad I am that our family is this much together.
> Somehow during this time I also have the job of drawing a diagram or blueprint of the ship we are sailing on, including the place on the ship where my sister and I are staying. It's a fairly large clipper ship. I label that area where my sister and I are staying with the word: "Heroines."

She felt very strong emotions when she woke and wrote the dream down, particularly when she wrote the words, "It's sort of a part of life." Before her father died, in his last months, he had experienced such failings in his bodily functions as the dream mentions, and she had done some of the cleaning up after him. Yet there seemed to her to be more to the dream than merely rehashing those experiences. It seemed more important. This image is reminiscent of one of the labors of Hercules, where he must clean out the foul accumulation of thirty years from the Augean stables.

As she began to work through each image of the dream, her own associations came as something of a shock to her. First, she understood the ship as suggesting that she was in connection with the unconscious, as represented by the water. She loved old clipper ships such as this, and it might be noted that they are moved by nature—the wind—not by mechanical means. This and the rural setting of the middle scene all suggest a close connection with the natural world.

However, when she asked herself the question "What mess did my father leave behind?" she knew it had to do with money. At first she could not connect this with the dream, but she knew that when she reflected on what kind of mess he left behind, it was about money.

She thought her father had always been absurdly tightfisted with money, though there was enough for comfortable living, even for a little legacy for his children. She thought he had made a great todo for years about "THE WILL." She also felt her mother had cheated herself in life by trading the possibility of autonomy for security. Neither she nor the sister in the dream had done so.

She then began to reflect on the various financial issues which her family, like most families, had to deal with. She herself always wanted to forget money, not to talk about it, so they could all stay close to each other and not fight—the feeling of closeness she had rejoiced about in the dream.

Yet the night before the dream, her sister had telephoned concerning a family situation about money, which she feared might become a "mess." The dreamer said she really feared, as she put it, "that the shit would hit the fan." These associations seemed to be moving closer to her father's mess that she was responsible for cleaning up.

She desperately wanted for the family cohesiveness to be maintained, yet she did not want it at the price of anyone becoming as tightfisted as she felt her father had been, nor as lifelimiting as she felt her mother had been. Interestingly, she and the sister in the dream were the two people who had worked hardest to "hold in with the family"—to support this cohesiveness—the very sister whose financial situation might now cause a breach.

In thinking more deeply about the family situation, she saw that the very thing she most feared—a breach in the family—might well be brought about by just the action she felt inclined to take: ignoring it and hoping it would go away. She herself associated this with wanting to be just her "father's daughter" in the sense of "Daddy's little girl" who doesn't "worry her pretty little head" about dirty old things like money. She saw in herself a real temptation to regress to just such a childish attitude.

Then she made one further association: she and her husband (to whom the telephone call in the dream was directed) had been working on a knotty financial matter the night before, *when her sister called!* She said neither she nor her husband were very good with money, but the night before he made her sit down for the two of them to work their problems through—and some of it was unpleasant. They had just finished working out a new "austerity budget" when her sister's telephone call came. She hated doing such tasks, but frequently was flooded with new energy when such a task was finished. As she put it, "Father's daughter *never* wants to do it!"

Her last association was with the fact that she had grey hair in the dream, contrary to waking fact. Her associations with grey hair were with someone who is sturdy, practical, reliable. The dream then became clear to her.

The end of the dream described to her what her task was to be: a diagram or blueprint of the ship in which she could "sail on." In order to clean up her father's mess, as it was left in her own patterns of behavior, she had to do just such sturdy, practical, detailed work.

Then, if she did so, the label to be placed on the area where she and her sister stayed was that of "heroines." It *was* a heroic task for her to make this change, and this insight was moving to her, especially because Joseph Campbell's hero book had been life-changing for her at a time when traditional spiritual answers had failed for her. She now saw this kind of responsibility as both heroic and energizing for her own future. Then she could probably bring this treasure back to her family as well, to help keep the cohesiveness she cherished for them all.

## Leadership

An engineer in his late twenties, whom we will call Rick, began to pay some attention to his dreams and his inner life out of a sense of frustration with the way his life was proceeding in several aspects.

The first dreams he remembered seemed to deal with his frustrations about the questions of his leadership ability and his relationship with his father. In the first dream that he remembered his father overheard Rick make a critical remark about the father. His father yelled angrily at him, "Why aren't you as successful as me?" Rick felt like a chastised little boy and woke up feeling terrible.

He wrote the dream down, reflecting about his experiences with his father during boyhood. His father had always pushed him to be a leader, but in areas in which his *father* was more interested than Rick. In areas Rick liked, such as making model airplanes, his father first pushed him with tasks too difficult for his age; and then when Rick mastered them with a lot of work and imagination, his father never had time to come watch them fly. Rick spent his Saturdays at the field alone, feeling that it was nearly impossible for him to get his father's interest.

As an adult, though he had a good job, he felt shy, not on the same "level" as his colleagues, not worthy of their time. At the time of the dream, he had just had a major performance evaluation at work, from which he got the same report he always received—low scores on leadership and responsibility. He seemed to be caught in the same frustration on the job which he had felt at home with his father. The thought of this made him very angry at himself, as well as at his father; and the next week, he had the following dream:

> There is a mission for me to perform—a spy type, or to rescue someone. I'm to accomplish part of the mission in a glider, so I take a practice flight. While trying to land, the plane won't go down, no matter how much control I give it. The nose is pointed so far down, only the straps are holding me in the seat. I get a miniature tail from somewhere and hold it out in the wind in front of me to give me better control. I finally land the plane, but it's 2:45, and I'm supposed to leave for the mission at 3:00. The glider has yet to be disassembled and put on a train for transport. Lots of worry because I'm late. Confused.
>
> A train is going fast through countryside. My vantage is as from a helicopter. A group of women are skilled in boarding the train while it is moving by lassooing part of the train with a rope, then they jump over a bridge, hanging on to the other end of the rope. The train pulls the rope taut and catapults a woman onto the train. I watch as five or so women perform their acrobatics, each with a different style.

It is easy to guess that Rick's mission is to rescue himself from the limitations in his own self-esteem; he has to spy out how to accomplish this mission. The glider practice is his beginning to unravel how his childhood complexes are still hampering the grown man. In the dream he felt as if he were being held up in the air while he tried to get down to earth. He said this felt much like his outer life. He always tried to plan too much, not thinking through the situations beforehand, and thus never accomplishing what he was scheduled to do. This in turn continually made him behave irresponsibly, which made him shyer than ever, so that he never requested help when he needed it. The first paragraph thus presents a visual image of his current behavior patterns.

The second paragraph, and the skilled accomplishments of the women he observes, may then present a visual image of what can be achieved. They get across a bridge by connecting themselves to the moving train and hanging on, each doing so in her own style. Rick is still removed from this action—only an observer—but the achievement of the women suggests that if he can get in touch with his own feminine, feeling strengths, he may be able to do his own acrobatics.

In another dream a week later he was in fact doing his own gymnastics in another dangerous situation, and the last sentence of that dream held out even more promise: "Once over the hill we break into a run, and I run joyfully cross-country down the hillside."

Rick had a lot of inner tasks to do in order to change himself and his inner vision of himself, but he stayed with the task, slowly but surely reassessing his ability and learning to be more responsible. Interestingly, though he had more or less forgotten this glider dream, he later learned hang-gliding as a sport and enjoyed the adult version of his youthful model airplanes. When we asked him for permission to use these dreams three years later, he was surprised to recall them and even more surprised to realize the contrast between his job situation in the three years.

The changes had come about so gradually that it took such a comparison to make him realize how far he had come. He had just been placed in charge of a major project at work, having learned more about being a leader and about his own worth than he had registered consciously. There were still a number of areas in his life with which he was not contented, but at work at least he had truly begun to bring "home" the competent leader he had now been able to "rescue."

## Being Stabbed Front and Back

The next dream contains both the crossing of the threshold and the danger encountered when the new world is entered:

> Three of us were swimming up a river. It became very shallow and dirty. I kept thinking it was too shallow to continue swimming; but we swam until we came to a wooden bridge with an enclosed shelter-recreation area on each end of the bridge. There were several workmen around the area. We entered one side, and I crossed over to the other side, alone. I didn't know where the others were, so I called them on the phone to let them know where I was. (It was a very short distance across the bridge.)
>
> While I was on the phone a man came toward me with a knife. I told the others I needed help, but I continued to act like I was talking, thinking he wouldn't do anything until the connection was broken. I was describing the situation and trying to keep calm when he attacked with the knife. I was stabbed many times, front and back. The friends and workmen came running immediately, but they were too late.
>
> My feeling—help was so near, and they still couldn't help.

This dream suggests that the dreamer is at a transition point in her life. At the beginning she is swimming with a group; note that she is swimming *up* the river—the hard way to go, to swim against the current. Her associations with this part of the dream were that she continued to swim though the water was too shallow and dirty because, "Well, the others were."

Then she comes to the transition moment: she crosses a bridge. This is an example of crossing the threshold. This motif is reinforced by the fact that she is suddenly alone. This is a lonely task, requiring bravery. She is uneasy with being alone and tries to telephone the others, who haven't come with her.

This part of the dream suggests that when she goes along with the crowd, operating with others against her better judgment, it is too shallow for her—she needs something deeper. This sense of needing something different had indeed been going on in her life at the time of the dream.

She was a sister in a religious order and had been for thirty-five years. She was in her mid-fifties and outwardly very successful. She had made a success of all the high-level administrative tasks she had

## The Road of Trials · 99

been assigned, though several of them were very difficult and painful for her. Through it all, she had kept smiling, though a deep discontentment had been growing in her. Finally, against the pattern of her order at the time, she simply told them she was resigning from her assigned job, though they pleaded with her to stay. In response to their pleas, she agreed to stay for six more months and tried to minister to her own needs in other ways. To her irritation, they did nothing about finding a replacement for her. Despite this, she continued to insist—a thing she had not done before.

This itself was a heroic move, and you might expect that the dream came at that time—with her trying to communicate with the "others" and being stabbed front and back. However, the dream did not come then. She did in fact stick to her guns. She did some training for a more pastoral kind of work and held a job using the new skills for a time. As a part of her training, her Clinical Pastoral Education group had criticized her for a "fake" smile, which they felt to be unreal and insincere. Her habit of trying to be agreeable and keep smiling was ingrained, but perhaps worn a little thin.

The dream came to her the next year, when she was faced with completing and filing a form for her order—a Mission Intent Form, saying what she wanted to do next (the order having modified their earlier pattern of assigning jobs without consulting the sisters).

Now she was faced with the new freedom for which she had fought, but she was very uncertain what it was she wanted to do. She could decide for herself, but what did she want? It was in this struggle to discern what was right for her to do next that the dream came. It picked up a motif of which she had become painfully aware: her sense of being alone. She then had to deal with a longstanding sense of loneliness, as well as the terrible freedom which God seems to give you to decide who you will become.

In this situation the dream shows vividly how it feels to be alone, deserted, unable to avoid making a decision, unable to avoid doing it alone. Help was so near in the dream, "but they were too late." She had to face the pain and danger of making a wrong decision all alone; there would be no one to blame but herself if she took a turning which made her miserable. In this sense, she had crossed the threshold and was facing her time of trials—or possible mutilation and pain from the stabbing knife.

Actually, in small and large ways, the mutilating attack was taking place. In small ways, for example, her own awesome efficiency was *not* shared by the other sisters she lived with: for example, her room sink stayed stopped up for six weeks; no one with power to do so got the television repaired for over a month; her closet door was hung askew and her door would not close—and *no one* would listen or support her, nor was she herself, in their convent organization, permitted to approach the parish pastor to see about repairs.

Her new training had begun to put her in touch with her old angers, her self-effacing (mealy-mouthed?) lack of assertion all her life; but the other sisters had not had her new training, and they were not where she was. So when she got angry over these small but annoying things, she would at once feel guilty and begin to "stab" herself with old opinions and "shoulds." "I *should* be more forgiving of others; I *shouldn't* be so selfish."

At the emotional level, she made one further association with the attack in the dream, which was much more serious. The dream came just after she read a newspaper story which had horrified her. The story concerned a policeman who, after being captured and tortured, called out so that neighbors could hear him, "Won't anyone help me?" And no one ever did; the policeman finally died at the hands of his torturers. The story haunted her, and her dream came the night after she read it.

This association suggests that the issue is a serious one for her. It is torture and maybe death for her (the dream ends on an ambivalent note) if she continues in her old pattern of smiling and giving in—if she retreats instead of moving bravely forward in new directions. In fact, she did make a brave decision and moved on to a new job. Three years later, when she wrote to give us permission to use this dream, she was in the new work and had carved out a personally fulfilling and socially useful niche for herself, which combined her administrative skills and her pastoral training. So in later years, she had brought the treasure home and was sharing it with the larger community in creative ways.

## Defining Boundaries

A creative and successful minister in his fifties was overcome with anxiety, which pushed him into doing some deep examination of his own destructive inner patterns. Though he felt very close to God and inspired many others to develop their own spirituality, he felt burned out, exhausted, and almost ready to quit. It seemed time for him to try to figure out where all his anxiety came from.

This was easy to see on a surface level. He never said no to any request for help; he overscheduled himself badly, ending up not being able to do all he had promised. He consistently arrived late for appointments because he could never leave the last place, and he felt guilty all the time (which drove him to work harder to try to make up for his own failures). He would literally lie awake night after night worrying about how he could help make things smoother for various people. Not surprisingly, his body had begun to reflect his anxiety through various illnesses. Unfortunately, this is all too familiar a story. He worked, as have many others, with some helpful ways of handling his stress. He began regular physical exercise, watched his diet, learned relaxation techniques. All this helped, but he still continued his same work patterns and thus his same anxieties.

It seemed as if he needed to know more about where these patterns came from in terms of his own history, and this examination proved instructive. There had been a normative family event when he was only a toddler. His next oldest sister died; and, as he put it, "My mother grieved for the rest of her life." A sensitive child, he took on the task of comforting his mother. He remembered fretting as a child because his father and others never gave his mother enough comfort, and he took on trying to make it all right with her. Since she remained a permanent griever, his task, or course, was impossible; but it almost seemed as if this early life experience left him a person without boundaries.

His empathic gifts made him a good listener for others, who received great comfort from his presence, but he himself had never learned to keep himself free from their pain. He took it into himself instead of leaving their pain with them and just being present to it—just as he had done with his mother when he was little. Inside himself he was always thinking, "What can I do to fix this?" Of course, he seldom could fix anything for another person, so he lived in the same frustration he must have felt as a little boy when his mother's grief went on and on. It was as if he did not even have a skin that separated him from others.

In theological terms he could see that he was trying to do the task which had already been done—saving people. Being God was too big a job even for as talented a pastor as he was! He could say this intellectually, but the pattern was so ingrained in him that he had great difficulty setting any limits on his pastoring.

He reported that he had one repetitive dream pattern for years: there is a test to be taken, and he cannot complete it for some reason. This felt like the same lack of ability to control the outcome which he constantly experienced. He finally began to realize, after receiving a particularly difficult request for help, that, as he put it, "I have to protect myself." About this time he had a significant dream, which he characterized as "very uncomfortable":

> It is the last day of boarding school. I remember all the desks, all the kids. The teacher gave an assignment for everyone to do a pictorial study and report. It seemed like an enormous job—too much going on besides this task. Everyone was trying to finish packing.
>
> I started copying a passage describing one character—seems to be a historical figure in an important geographical study. I was upset with the teacher for assigning it and figured I couldn't finish the task. I had to get the car ready for the trip—maybe rent a car big enough for all of us. One student, a girl, "wanted" to commit suicide. I called the teacher's assistant out of class to tell her about the student. The student's intent wasn't very serious.

The dream spells out his task specifically. It is in the repetitive pattern of a number of his dreams. Such repetition always indicates a pressing issue to be dealt with. This time his task is a "geographical" one—surely having to do with learning to set boundaries. He needs boundaries between himself and the pain of others; he needs boundaries on how much he agrees to do; he needs boundaries on his time and energy. The dream shows the frustration the potential hero frequently feels. The task feels like too much; the dreamer feels he cannot possibly finish the task.

There is even a part of him, represented by the anima-figure student who "wants" to commit suicide, who wants to quit and throw it all up, but even in the dream he knows that the intention to quit by suicide is not very serious.

As with many dreams, this one and some other task dreams he had about the same time helped give him energy to engage his patterns seriously, albeit somewhat grudgingly. The dream promises that the intent to quit and give up is not too serious, and subsequent dreams affirmed the fact that he can ask for assistance and get it as he plods through his geographical work.

### John Wayne to the Rescue

A powerful series of dreams over a two-year period came to a middle-aged woman whom we will call Kathleen. After her children left home, she began a new career as a counselor. The first two dreams came near each other, the first dream combining some ordinary images with archetypal ones, perhaps best summarized in the anomalous setting—a cave with indirect lighting:

> I was in a large cave which was pretty well lighted with indirect lighting. I was lying in a bed with Marla. The bed had short rails around it like a baby bed. We saw a dirt crusted stick begin to move. It was a snake. As it began to move out of the earth, the earth opened up like a birth canal, and the snake got bigger and bigger until it was the size of a dinosaur. It slid down into the water next to Marla. It was attracted to her because she was menstruating. We were scared.
>
> I asked how we could be saved. A voice told us the snake ate pigs and cows. "Alive?" I asked, "Yes." I asked why the snake was not killed rather than sacrificing the pigs and cows alive. The owner of the voice seemed to have the power to make that decision.
>
> We moved our meeting to a house down the street to get away from the snake. I was acting president, but got no money for it. Someone said I did a good job.

This dream contains one of the better reasons to move a meeting we have ever seen! The last paragraph is the one which has the more ordinary symbolism, and most of it refers directly to her current situation. If the symbolism is taken as a part of her inner world, she *is* the "acting president," which implies that she is not really permanently in charge. This certainly seemed true to her. Furthermore, she worried continually over money for her services, as do many beginning counselors, especially women, who frequently have a hard time valuing what they do. Yet it was also true that she actually "did a good job" of her work, even though she herself had difficulty valuing it.

In the other, more obscure symbolism of the dream, there are many feminine images, such as the birth canal, menstruation, and even, in her personal associations, the pigs and cows, whom she thought of as "sweet, tame, domesticated farm animals." The snake comes out of the birth canal, which is in a cave. In the material world caves are like the womb of the ground, which is itself an archetypal symbol of the feminine, the *mater*, Mother Earth, that out of which life is born.

Marla was an old friend from first grade and a person Kathleen considered a "success story" in the way she had lived her life fully and well. They are together in a baby bed, implying that she is at a "baby" stage in this aspect of her life. The snake as the chthonic symbol of some new challenge of awareness seemed terrifying to her, and this in turn seemed like the terror she sometimes felt in accepting her new authority as a counselor.

The dream seems to say that if she cannot deal with her fright at this new awareness or enlargement of her personality which the snake challenges her to, then the snake can turn into a dinosaur and swallow alive these feminine symbols. Somehow she needs to claim a professional side of herself in a new way.

Three days later, she dreamed:

> I was with a lot of people in an old Western saloon. I was in charge until a man came in with a huge whip and began snapping it around.

This dream swings around to the other side. She had been dealing with the contrast between helplessness and authority the week before, and this dream has another image of what happens to authority which gets out of control. It is as if a wild, aggressive masculinity takes over. She said the image she had of the scene in the dream was like movies where the only people in western saloons were men and prostitutes, and they all got drunk and fought. Her animus got loose in this dream and acted out a movie scene.

She worked hard on changing her attitudes into a more integrated pattern, and she had another cave dream two years later:

> A Chinese girl, May Ling, tall and slim and beautiful, was seeking wisdom so that she would feel safe and secure. Her husband (not Chinese) was also tall, slim, and handsome. They lived on the ocean which was clear green, and the beach was white sand and beautiful.
> She was going to give birth in a large cave-like place, and I prepared

the place for this by covering a large flat rock with a big, blue cloth. I knew I didn't know how to deliver a baby without someone to help me who had experience, so hoped she/he would come help with the birth. It was in an area of huge dark rocks. She was out in the water (ocean), standing on a sunken bathtub waiting for a boy to deliver a proverb (wise message).

He came and was naked (about 16 years old) and was sitting in a chair-like tub in the water. He sat so that his genitals were very visible, hoping to distract her. He handed her a note. She goes back to the sand to give birth.

In her associations Kathleen said in the dream she was not sure whether the Chinese girl or she herself was to give birth. She had been doing some spiritual study and felt she was "coming alive spiritually"—this was her association with giving birth. Chinese for her meant "foreign" and, as the dream suggests, wisdom.

She was coming into "foreign country" in her efforts to change her lifelong patterns of passivity and nurturing others to the exclusion of her own needs. May Ling, her alter-ego shadow in the dream, still wanted safety and security, but she also sought wisdom. The young boy comes to help, yet his emphasis on his sexuality is seen in the dream as a distraction which can hinder the new birth, even though he does bring the wise proverb she needs. It would take wisdom and not getting distracted, as well as staying firmly grounded, to give birth to her new possibilities.

Two months later her help arrived in a strong form:

I was to be in a race with Jo (my dog). We met in a shopping center. I knew some of the people and talked with them, went to the rest room, and came back to line up. Our female partner took us to our starting place with leash and dog.

During the race I had to help Jo over barriers and didn't keep her leashed much. I didn't know if I could finish the race, since it had been so hard last year. Once we passed a box of leashes and later I wished I had taken one since I couldn't keep track of Jo, but it was hard to run with her on a leash.

I ran up by the hall where they were having a party, but the race wasn't over, so finished the race and went back to the party.

I had been told earlier that John Wayne would be my sponsor. Now he showed up. I thought this strange since I didn't know him. He suggested we go to the party, and he held my hand. I suppose he did this so everyone would think we were old friends. It made me feel good.

She was very moved by the end of this dream, felt that it was important, and almost cried when she told about John Wayne holding her hand. She felt "patronized," but not in the negative sense—rather as if she had a patron to help her, support her, and affirm her. It was a wonderful dream for her.

Her dog Jo is an interesting aspect of the dream, as an aspect of herself in a less differentiated way. Jo had been "put to sleep" the year before because of illness and pain. Kathleeen said Jo had been "a real sweetheart" whose whole life was based on trying to please people. Jo was always good and always doing whatever you needed her to do.

Actually, this was not a bad description of Kathleen herself—good traits, but not when overdone at too much cost. The race which needed to be run was like her counseling practice, which continued to prosper, but about which she sometimes felt considerable anxiety. The leash is an important part of the imagery, perhaps suggesting that Kathleen tended to put a leash on her own instincts and emotions, which made the race very hard to run. She feared she would not be able to finish the race, because "it had been so hard last year."

Yet this year she does finish, which reflected her improvement. Her associations with John Wayne were: stable, reliable, good guy, big and strong. She did not agree with some of his right-wing opinions, but otherwise admired his strength, ability, and his saying what he thought. He is a stronger helper by far than the naked sixteen year-old, and his help enables her to go to the party with a feeling of belonging. His holding her hand was like an integrating of these traits of his into her Jo side.

As a therapist, she felt that she could not be a John Wayne without the Jo side. Otherwise, she might be like the whip snapper in the saloon dream. If she does integrate these two parts of herself and run the race, then she gets to go to the party. In her disagreement with some of John Wayne's politics, there may remain the suggestion that her animus or masculine side requires further development to the socialization of her integrated way of being. Her animus is still too conservative to express her value system, and her feminine side is still undifferentiated at the human level. The dream encourages her achievement, but also points the way for continued work.

These examples are only suggestions, of course, of the multiplicity of tests and tasks which confront the human spirit on the road. As has been suggested, the specific actions and images in each dream are to be examined for their connection with the dreamer's current life to see how this trial is being presented to the dreamer and sometimes also how the dreamer is responding to the challenge so far. For example, many people dream they have to take a test, but they cannot find the place where the test is to be given, or they forgot to read the book, or they did not even know they were taking the class until the examination time arrived. Each such theme, as well as the more archetypal ones, can be related to the dreamer's life. Once the dream challenge is understood, then it is the dreamer's responsibility to respond to it.

# ▶10

# Rites of Passage

Just as some have thought that life could be demythologized and that symbols could pass away as science discovers more about the material world, so some have also thought that ritual was dead. We think both of these views are shortsighted and inaccurate.

Ritual, like myth and symbol, has a purpose of its own. If the meaning of old rituals is gone, a new ritual will be produced or grow up in each community. In fact, with the demise of most initiation rites in contemporary society the psyche of individuals today often resorts to dream imagery. The dreams produce ritual imagery when the dreamer is ready to move from one status to another.

Religious and community rituals in all cultures mark times of transition; in traditional cultures there is ritual response to the individual's need to mark major transformations. There are rituals of birth, coming of age, marriage, vocation, reconciliation, healing, parenting, and death, the ultimate frontier. As we have suggested, each of these, as well as many smaller increments of consciousness and growth, can be seen as fitting the hero journey grid. Such rituals codify the separation, trials, and return.

Mircea Eliade has said that "the nostalgia for initiatory scenarios" is indicated by the many initiation themes found in so many contemporary literary and artistic creations.[1] T. S. Eliot's poem "The Waste Land" is one obvious example; that complicated poem is perhaps best understood by a combination of the study of initiation rites (as Eliot himself stated) and a study of dream interpretation.[2] Much of modern literature and art portray this common longing for renewal as part of the human experience. Growth, as someone has said, is the evidence of life.

Initiation rituals have traditionally marked the movement from one status to another; and one commonly thinks of those rites which traditionally are observed upon coming of age, when youth are incorporated into the adult community. Psychologically, these are associated with the strengthening of the ego for adult tasks. Initiatory experiences are not, however, limited to the psychology of youth. The ego needs strengthening and encouragement at transition moments throughout life. The midlife crisis, about which much has been written, is one prominent such time; the movement from middle age to old age also calls for some recognition by the ego of a changed situation in life. Joseph Henderson writes, "At these critical periods, the archetype of initiation is strongly activated to provide a meaningful transition that offers something more spiritually satisfying than the adolescent rites with their strong secular flavor."[3] Evelyn Eaton Whitehead and James D. Whitehead have spelled out aspects of this need in their book *Christian Life Patterns: The Psychological Challenges and Religious Invitations of Adult Life*.[4]

Henderson also points out that, as a general rule, hero symbols arise when the ego needs additional help—when, as he says, "the conscious mind needs assistance in some task that it cannot accomplish unaided or without drawing on the sources of strength that lie in the unconscious mind."[5] Jung's path of individuation, involving, as it does, confrontation and assimilation of the shadow and contrasexual aspects of the personal psyche, is, as we have suggested, another way of describing the hero journey with its road of trials.

The adult quest entails a gradual development in appreciation of what lies within. Dreams which herald such important moments frequently come in archetypally ritualistic forms, with super powers coming in aid of the dreamer or with ancient patterns of tasks to be accomplished.

## Coming of Age

One super power entered the dream of a fourteen-year-old boy the night after he had argued unpleasantly all evening with his father over the best way to accomplish a mechanical task which needed doing at their house—a task about which they disagreed:

> A boy saw Big Foot, and he had a camera with him and began to take pictures of Big Foot and follow him. Then he and a group were on a cliff, and Big Foot threw the boy's father off the cliff.

We know little else about the dreamer's associations, but the symbols are fairly self-explanatory. The boy had experienced frustration and powerlessness with his father's (as he saw it) misguided opinions. His father no longer seemed infallible to him in the way fathers frequently do to young children, but he himself had been unable to change his father's mind.

The energy for the separation from the father and the desire to be powerful and effective came in the person of Big Foot, the larger-than-life powerhouse whose picture he took and whom he decided to "follow." The destruction of the idealized father is vividly portrayed by his new super-power helper, so the death portion of the death-rebirth cycle is shown in the dream (an archetypal movement similar to that which Freud identified as the Oedipal slaying of the father), with the boy's own rebirth as a man still to come. The ritual of achieving adulthood is provided in the energy of the dream, and thus the boy got one increment of the energy needed for the separation into his own manhood.

## Purification

A dream of purification came to one woman shortly after her thirty-fifth birthday. The dream labels the action as an initiation ritual:

> It was as though I was in the town where I was born [in the rural western United States], but the atmosphere was dark and mysterious. This seemed to be an initiation ritual—or party.
>
> I was with my mother and another girl, and Emma Scruggs (a neighbor who lived down the street when I was growing up) seemed to be there. The girl and I were discussing what protection we'd use. I said I had already taken care of that. The protection had to do with how we would take care of ourselves during our periods so we wouldn't be so vulnerable.
>
> My mother was surprised and taken aback. I wanted to explain that she need not be suspicious; that I'd barely started my period—and made a mental note to tell her sometime when we were alone.

Part of the process meant diving into a pool from a room high above it. It was a purification pool. I made the dive and was climbing the ladder back—not to the room but skyward—when I had these thoughts of my mother. The climb was a little frightening. I wished I hadn't had to do it all alone—but realized I was going to make it safely after all—just a few more steps to go. My hair was long and wet and I was clothed in a white robe.

Again there were thoughts about telling my mother about my period. There was the image of a small cross of red on a sanitary napkin and the thought that my period was just a day long. I wished my mother knew these things—not knowing, it was as though she thought me more worldly than I was. I wondered if she would understand; if she would believe me if I told her.

The setting of the dream threw her back to her youthful home, where she had been close to nature in the open terrain, which she explored on foot and horseback. When she thought of being there, she remembered a feeling of contentment. In fact, during an adult depression, she had pasted in her journal pictures of herself as a gleeful child to remind herself that she had once known how to be happy.

At the time the dream came, she had stopped therapy and was seriously considering several major life transitions, some of which she had begun. She was still at her old job, however, postponing her new work, but making some moves to bring change to pass.

Emma Scruggs was an interesting figure from her childhood. She was a person spoken of as being from "the other side of the tracks"—fat, homely, earthy—but somehow compelling to the young dreamer. She said when she thought of Emma, she could remember watching her out of the corner of her eye and wondering what she was up to. Emma carried for the dreamer an aura of sexual secrets.

Obviously, at thirty-five she is far beyond the onset of menstruation, but her association with menarche was the memory of her mother's saying, "Congratulations on becoming a woman." She had liked it that her mother said this to her, but also felt confused at the time because she and her mother, as she put it, "weren't related in a way that would enable us to talk about womanhood and sexuality." She added that she often felt "vulnerable" during her periods even to the present, especially if the rest of her life was trying at the time.

Significantly, she also felt "vulnerable" much of the time when she was around her mother.

Her mother often regarded her with suspicion and had done so all her life. She said that after her own work in therapy she had come to understand the reason for this—that her own life, unlike her mother's life, had reflected a relationship to the feminine and to the unconscious that her mother was unable to understand—but, she added, "This is a heady way of saying what took a long time to feel."

She said her mother's suspicion had made it hard for the dreamer to be at ease with her own sexuality, which created a lot of inner conflict, because, at the same time, she seemed to know instinctively that her sensuality was a gift—perhaps represented in the dream by the presence of the instinctual Emma Scruggs. Reflecting on this time in her life, she noted: "As I think now about growing up in the arms of mother nature, I'm flooded with sense perceptions of what that was like: the fragrance of the animals and their softness, the smell of manure and straw, seeing my colts born and being licked off by their mothers—the list could go on and on. No wonder it was so hard to carry this past my mother into puberty and into womanhood. Doing so is what the dream is about."

She also wondered whether her mother, too, might have been a very passionate person in her own right, though she probably got little help in celebrating that part of herself. Thus her mother's suspicion might have also been partly envy, wanting to know what made her daughter so appealing as a woman.

She saw the dive into the pool for purification as representing what remained to be done. The pool reminded her of the Jewish ritual of mikvah, the purification bath for a woman after menses. Though not Jewish herself, she said she always found this a beautiful idea—not that woman is dirty and needs to be cleansed, but that she can honor the way her body relates her to the cycles of the earth and the moon.

Her ritual dive into the purification pool can be further amplified by the general ritual symbolism of water, as elaborated by Leonel Mitchell:

> "Passing through the waters" is always symbolic of death and rebirth. This is true both of individual rites of initiatory washing and of great cosmic myths, such as the flood, the crossing of the River Styx by the

souls of the departed, or the passage of the Red Sea by Moses and the Israelites. What went before is dissolved. Entry into the waters marks a temporary return to formlessness, as when the Spirit of God brooded over the waters of chaos at the dawn of creation. To emerge from the waters is to reenact the creation of the cosmos from the waters of chaos. It is the beginning of a new existence.[6]

That the cross, a symbol of wholeness, should appear on a sanitary napkin was instructive for her. She said she was still, even at her age, embarrassed to purchase them, and she remembered her frustration when her mother would not explain what they were one day when she first ran across a box. Coupled with her worry in the dream over how worldly her mother thought her to be, these elements of worry in the dream point to the nature of the change she needs to make.

It is as if she has, at least in part, internalized some of her mother's opinions about the feminine, and this remnant needs to be transcended for her to be fully at one with herself. She said her mother for a long time thought her to be more experienced sexually than she really was, mistakenly attributing sensual appreciation for sexual activity. You might say that her mother concretized the experience of the feminine into sexual behavior—as much of our culture does today.

Since, in the dream, she "wished my mother knew these things," the dream suggests that her mother-in-her also somehow does not know "these things." The dream closes on an unfinished note. Will the purification of the attitude toward the feminine be completed and understood? Will it be believed? Will the ritual white robe of purity be accepted on a continuing basis?

There is a promise of success in that, despite the fright of "climbing the ladder back," she also "realized I was going to make it safely after all." There are "just a few more steps to go."

It seems that the dream takes her back to her place of childhood joy to remind her that this initiation will also be a party. Then it presents her worries in the person of her mother, who worried—not accurately—about her femininity. Since she did feel joy as a child in that setting and since she knows that her mother's worries were untrue, she can realize that the worries she is currently having about herself are also untrue. Further, she can escape from them by claiming her purification ritual. She can use the image of her childhood innocence to claim the innocence of her present ability to achieve her present tasks.

As she put it, the dream "speaks not only of initiation, but of purification, atonement, at-one-ment. Though so newly come into womanhood (personhood?), I'm feeling at-one. It's as though there's been a karmic release and I'm free—from the hurt, vulnerability, and resentment that held me back from life."

## Baptism

The next dream used the symbols of baptism, a wall, and death to speak to the dreamer about her relationship to the church:

> I am repairing a concrete wall. A dear woman friend comes to me and asks to be buried under the last section of wall. I am almost to that section, and I say, "Yes." Then I realize that she is dying. Someone has left a pair of slippers there. I feel it is a symbol of baptism, but also realize it can mean death. As I start to work on the wall, I ask her to come talk to me. There are several tables of people eating—like a cafe—and they move so she can be close to me. An overwhelming sense of gratitude and sadness comes over me.
>
> I wake up feeling so sad, and the feeling is still strong.

She said the feeling of sadness was so strong that she was in tears most of the day. At the time of the dream, she was far from the traditional baptismal age. She was sixty years old and a "cradle Catholic," to whom the church had always been central. She said she had been thrilled by Vatican II and the changes it promised, but at the time of the dream disenchantment had taken over. Though she still made regular retreats and longed to be a faithful daughter of the church, she found it too often to be "back to the Middle Ages." She still went to church "because it's law, but the liturgy is so bad it's hell to go." She felt angry at priests who were responsible for such liturgies and for the lack of freedom in the church.

As she worked with the dream, she associated the "last section of the wall," which was at the corner with "turning a corner"—some change or new direction. She then thought the dream concerned turning a corner in the sense of "working on the last section of my life." The unknown woman in the dream inspired great love in her, and she felt her to represent some loving, free, spirited, hopeful part of herself—as she put it, "the dearest part of me, what I have wanted to be." She did not want that woman to be buried under the wall, and the symbols of baptismal slippers and eating at the tables seemed to offer an alternative ending.

After several efforts at active imagination about the wall and the woman, she associated the wall with the church. It has been for her both a barrier and a support, a confinement and a shelter. She had depended on it all her life, yet it was in bad repair. It enclosed her in familiar surroundings. The woman was the loyal part of her, true to the church, feeling safe there because she felt God was there. If she kept on repairing the wall, the woman would be dead and buried under it. It seemed to her—difficult and dark as that way seemed—that she must stop repairing the wall and simply sit down with the woman and eat together. When she became bitter at the church, she hurt this loyal, naive, and innocent part of herself.

She felt that for her own soul's health she needed to find some way to accept the limitations of the wall without coming to hate it. She needed to grow up, incorporating these two parts of herself—turning the naivete and innocence into wisdom and strength. The baptismal slippers were both a symbol of some newness of life and a symbol of comfort, as slippers are comfortable to wear.

She had been a fearful person all her life, and the seeking she was engaged in had led her into places that seemed empty. Yet she received from the ritual symbols in this dream the courage to see that God was also in the emptiness, in the void. She could seek true holiness in the dark, holding the hand of the loving woman shadow friend.

## Anointing for Healing

The next dreamer was a young pastor who was taking specialized training in pastoral counseling while also serving a local church. He was a formal person who had realized that he was formal in part as a defense against vulnerability. He was the misfit in his family of origin—the one who was different and harshly judged by the others because of that difference. After a wounding experience in one church he served, he became even more defensive. Some work in a supervision group showed him that he was perhaps refusing the next step on his hero journey because of his fears.

His fears surfaced as he prepared to face the Staff Support Committee of his church toward the end of his probationary period. Then he had this dream:

> My Supervisor performs a healing ritual on me after group supervision, which was in a motel-hospital room. Her husband is there too. She instructs me to rip off my shirt and pour water on my chest. But then she does it for me. I lie down on a bed, push the covers aside, and she dribbles water and orange juice on me.
>
> Then I am helping clean up, standing near her husband, talking with him about being outdoors. My daughter comes in to leave with me, and I tell her to wait so I can offer to pay my Supervisor.

Here the dream itself labels this odd ritual as a healing ritual, and it takes place in a (part) hospital, which is a place of healing. The setting also is partly a motel, which is in his association a stop on a journey and a place of transition. All these elements point to the dream as a positive transition for him.

The people in the dream are also positive for him. His supervisor had helped him to a more positive image of himself by her affirmation—the affirmation so sadly lacking in his childhood. She and her husband seemed to him a kind of wisdom couple, who represented a gentle guiding toward having the courage to face his initiation into being a new person.

The water and orange juice were for him "liquids of anointing," like oil and water, but the orange juice instead of oil suggested the sun, the golden fluid of the masculine. He thus felt anointed for healing in the dream by the affirming wise couple with the healthy fluids of nature and masculinity.

Talking with the husband about the outdoors carried this feeling forward for him. As the husband moved into the foreground of the dream, it seemed as if he were being called forth into the freedom and peace of the outdoors in a manly way. This was a new and good feeling for him, since his own father and brothers disdained his way of being.

His daughter, who comes in at the end of the dream, is the person most like him and so seemed to represent a new anima possibility by the fact that she was going with him. His associations with paying his supervisor were "closure, completion, ritual acknowledgment."

The dream's positive encouragement gave him new energy for self-acceptance. His continued work was affirmed again in a dream about six weeks later in which another ritual of healing occurred. There he had a positive, loving experience with the man who had been a major source of his wounding at his former church. In the dream he felt no animosity at all toward the man, and he experienced this as a sign that he had in fact entered his hero journey even to the integration of this hated shadow figure. His dream rituals were truly healing for him.

## Sacrifice

A devoted church worker had the following dream the night after attending a meeting of the women of the church, of which she was a regional officer:

> I was imprisoned in a Nazi compound. Sometimes it was like a building; at other times it was like a community and the hallways became streets.
> I and those with me knew that I was scheduled for execution, but I do not know for what reason.
> In the time before the executioners came I bade a very loving farewell to my son. (In recalling it, it seems more like bidding a farewell to a lover than to a son.) He wanted to give me his blanket which he had in the front of his shirt so that I might be wrapped in it at my death. But I showed him that I, too, had one in the front of my shirt and that would be adequate. I was concerned that he would need his for warmth in the days to come.
> Then I bade my husband farewell. We held one another closely and passionately. I do not recall if I was still in his arms when the executors [*sic*] came or not.
> When they arrived I somehow knew the leader to be a much more compassionate man. He seemed regretful to be carrying out his task. He brought with him a wooden container. I knew even before he explained it was to hold my blood. I leaned over it and someone neatly cut my throat. I was surprised how little blood there was. I sat up and looked out the window. (It was like the window of the study where we used to live.) Everything began to grow very pale in color. I commented on it, and the man in charge said that was typical. Then he explained that he used the throat-cutting because it was terribly expensive using "Mace" which seemed to be the method used before. I

puzzled over that but everything was so pale I couldn't figure it out. I wondered if they had spared my husband the trauma of watching me killed.

Then I was walking along the north side of our house with a woman who was familiar. Everything was very pale.

I kept wondering why I hadn't died. I had, but I hadn't. I felt no pain, no fear. I recall feeling I must pray and did so, simply turning to the Lord in a natural and comfortable and trusting way, feeling he would take care of whatever.

In the dream itself I was trying to figure out its meaning and telling myself I must remember and write it down.

One other thing: a wooden casket was there. I'm not sure if my blanket was in it, but it seems so. I recall thinking if I would get in it to die others would not have to lift me in. But somehow I could not manage it.

In reflecting on this dream, she remembered that the last time she had dreamed of Nazis was also at the time of a churchwomen's board meeting. Nazi to her meant exclusivity, superiority, elitism to the extermination of all else. At the board meeting she had felt very opposed to one proposal, judging it to be elitist. She herself was much more dedicated to social action and personal growth, but this dream shocked her into the realization that she herself was feeling superior and elitist in opposition to the proposal. She wrote in her journal: "I realize I must guard against those traits in myself. Or perhaps guard against is the wrong phrase! I must recognize those things in myself and allow them to be put to death."

She did not fully comprehend the sacrificial, ritual aspect of the bloodletting, but could not forget the power of the dream. A year later she worked with prayer and journaling again about the dream; and this time it came to her that another aspect of the sacrifice had to do with her relationship with her son and her husband. In an imaginative dialogue with her son in her journal, she felt his nature—impulsive, outgoing, impractical, brash. She felt as if that part of herself was being put to death all the time. The dream came to suggest to her that she needed to be set free from the lid she always kept on her creativity, her sexuality, her dreams and hopes. In her prayers to her "Divine Executioner" she began to claim some kind of new life to be carried forth after her sacrificial death. This change may even be suggested in her "Freudian slip" in writing her dream. The second time she "means" to refer to her executioners. She instead calls them "executors." An executor is one who handles an estate under a will, not one who kills. They are thus connected with what happens after death.

General amplification of the dream image of her loss of blood points to the biblical understanding that "the blood is the life." As Mitchell says, "Blood is an important ritual image. Its symbolism is always life, not death."[7] The work this dreamer did is like receiving a saving blood transfusion; there is a promise of new life.

## Confession

A ritual dream of confession and blessing for ministry came to a woman in her forties. She was married, with children, a faithful church member all her life—a traditional suburban homemaker. In midlife, however, she became depressed and unhappy. She sought help from a spiritual director and in a small group which met regularly for prayer and study. She had begun to help others, though she still failed to recognize the strong level of leadership and ministry of which she was capable.

She felt somewhat dependent on the help of others, and then there was a worrisome development. Her spiritual director was leaving the city, and her small group was going to stop meeting. At this point she had a long dream which woke her at 2:00 A.M.:

> I was visiting a friend in Massachusetts. We were at a party in a penthouse, a very exclusive place. Then I went downstairs to a small, very exclusive dress shop like Saks. There was one section, beautifully decorated with a manikin dressed in beautiful clothes. I noticed how lush and thick the carpeting was.
>
> I thought about the people who worked here: "How can people stand spending their lives in such a tiny, circumscribed area? A corner like this that you are responsible for? Day after day, the same corner. You have to stay there and wait for people to come to you."
>
> Then, as though answering my own question, I thought: "You get used to it and don't even mind it—the same way you get used to having your 'world' be the house and suburb." I met and talked to the saleswomen, and they guided me back to the place I was going.
>
> Then my friend took me to see her father's old office; he was a doctor. The rooms were huge and shining-clean. We looked out across the meadows into beautiful countryside. I thought the building was deserted, but then people appeared—men, women, and children all dressed in strange, old-fashioned clothes, like Amish people. Somehow I knew they were a small, almost forgotten religious sect. My

friend wanted me to leave, as though it were embarrassing to her to have them around. I didn't want to leave.

They were speaking German, which I couldn't understand. I was struck by a longing and a compelling urge to go up to the leader and ask him to bless me. I knelt before him and with utter trust put both my hands in his and asked him to bless me. It was evidently very out of the ordinary for an "outsider" to do this, and the others protested.

But the leader looked into my eyes and smiled at me, then he looked over my head at the others and silenced them with his glance. He took my hands in his and silently and very gently pulled them out, until they were stretched out like a figure on a cross. I bowed low in reverence, and he murmured a blessing and (I think) a prophecy over me. I was swept with joy and a deep feeling of fulfillment. It was strange and very moving—I was stirred down to my depths.

I kept rejoicing inside myself that I had followed my leading and my own inclination to plead for the blessing—in spite of my friend's and the people's remonstrances—and despite the usual barrier in myself of shyness and reserve.

They gave me a red apron with a pocket in it. The pocket stretched horizontally across the entire front on the apron. It was, I was given to understand, a ceremonial and symbolic garment of the people. They tied it around my waist. In the pocket was a metal (pewter or silver) instrument of some sort. It was about 5 inches long—the bottom part was a spiral of concentric circles, large at the bottom, smaller at the top. The top part was (I think) a 2-pronged fork.

My friend returned and took me to her house. In the house were her father, his wife, her father's daughter by another woman, and the daughter's child, a girl of about 11. The daughter was worried about the behavior of the child—"afraid she's going to turn out bad."

I asked some question, and it was like lighting a match to a fuse of dynamite. The story of incest came out—of the father with the daughter—the result was the 11-year-old child. Somehow I had been the catalyst that brought this to light.

The father's wife finds all this out for the first time. It is like one explosion, then another. I don't like being there, but think "they ARE finding out why they had felt resentment and hatred (especially the stepmother for her stepdaughter)." She had "sensed" something, but had never been able to determine the cause.

The father, in bathrobe, comes in. He has been an invalid for years. (The thought goes through my mind "he's been sick because he's been keeping all this a secret for so long.")

I find out that the two women are Catholics and say in a tone of confrontation and authority, "How long has it been since you received the Sacraments of the Church?" The daughter says, "Since this happened." The stepmother can't take communion because she hates the stepdaughter and child. I say to her, "How long has it been since you've been to Confession?"

The daughter begins to weep. Gently I go to her, take her hands in mine, and kneel before her, looking in to her eyes, "Don't you know that's what I *do*? I help people find their way back to the Sacraments."

I know that now they have brought this out there is no need to hide any longer. They can go to Confession, find the forgiveness of God through absolution, receive Communion, and begin afresh . . . something good will happen. It is as though they "catch" something of my own assurance and joy of the creative possibilities of what has taken place.

We are then gathered, and all these people appear to see me off—the strange religious sect, the family, the people from the party—to wish me well and tell me that the brief contact they had with me was for good. Somehow it changed their lives. Someone puts a large leather brief case into the cab; it is a gift for me. It is full of papers that I can look at and study on the train.

Everyone is happy and joyful and grateful—they keep "making over me" as we go to catch the train.

The dream was obviously an important one, and she worked with it herself and with her spiritual director. She had been studying the psychology of C. G. Jung for about a year, but it still seemed somewhat like the German in the dream, which she could not understand.

Her associations with the setting in Massachusetts were that it was an intellectual place. The penthouse was high and intellectual. The dress shop she associated, as the dream itself suggests, with the restrained, narrow feminine life lived in her suburb. It had come to seem limited to her in this same way.

The strange, "almost forgotten" religious sect she related to her own inner life. In her active church work, she had almost lost touch with the inner meaning of her religion until her own distress had pushed her to seek help. Her spiritual director and the study she had been engaged in had led her to some almost forgotten pathways of Christian experience.

The blessing she sought and received from the leader is clearly named in the dream as *her* way to fulfillment and joy. Even though many others do not understand, and even though she herself usually feels shy and reserved, she is being called—and blessed—by this inner way. She is dressed for an outward sign of the blessing and also given a new "instrument." Is it stretching too far to see the instrument—circular at one end and pointed at the other—as a coming together of the feminine and masculine potential within her?

At any rate, she is immediately led into a place where a family has terrible hidden secrets and where her ministry to them is electric and immediate. She herself defines what this ministry is—"that's what I *do*." She and they are filled with joy at what she has to teach and offer them of the healing power of sacraments. (She herself, by the way, was not a Roman Catholic, but honored the sacraments.)

The joy everyone feels at the end was a strong encouragement for her to proceed with some new direction in her life. In the years that followed she did so. Though there were many dark times and many ordeals to overcome, she eventually became a counselor and a blessing to many in her city, even as the dream rituals foretell.

She had received a call to adventure, enforced by a ritual blessing and an exercise of her power for healing, and through all her subsequent trials, she remained true to her call and blessing.

## Ordination

One of the most remarkable dreams and subsequent synchronicities we have seen came to a man over thirty years before he gave us the dream to use. He had the dream in 1954. He was living in Milwaukee at the time, and his fiancée was living in Denver. She was taking the train to Chicago to visit him, and the night before her arrival, he was excited about her visit.

That evening he had a profound dream, which he felt required some knowledge of the Roman Catholic church in pre–Vatican II days to understand. He said that in those days in his church the faithful would approach the altar rail, kneel down, take the altar cloth and hold it under their chins, and the priest would distribute communion by walking up and down the altar rail, each time saying to the communicant, "Corpus domine nostra Jesu Christe, custodium anima in vita eternam meum, amen" (May the body of our Lord Jesus Christ preserve your soul to life everlasting, amen). With this background explanation, he described his dream:

> In the dream I was attending the sacrifice of the mass (as it was called in those days), and it was communion time. I approached the communion rail with the faithful, kneeled down, and waited for the priest to give me communion. As he approached me, giving communion to those kneeling next to me, he would pass me by, not giving me communion. The people would get up, go back to their pew, and new people would come and kneel down and receive, but each time the priest would pass me by. This caused a feeling of embarrassment, confusion and unworthiness in me.
>
> Finally, I was left kneeling there alone and in disgrace, got up and returned to my pew. I buried my face in my hands in prayer and confused wonderment when I looked up towards the altar and saw this brilliant person, a white haired priest in vestments holding the ciborium with communion in it. As I gazed upon this priest, he approached me—not walking, but just moved in the air towards me until his entire being, with the eucharist, entered into my being and we became one. I was elated with great joy. So much so, that I woke up and could not return to sleep as the joy was so immense. I did not understand the dream, but relished the peace and spiritual contentment that was derived from it.

Eagerely he drove to Chicago the next morning to meet his fiancée, and as was their custom, they walked from the railroad station to the Cathedral of Saint Francis to give a prayer of thanks for being together again and for a safe trip. As they walked toward the church, he told his fiancée about the dream with great excitement and gratefulness, but also confusion. As he was talking, he recounts, they passed a religious goods store, and in the window, hanging in a prominent place, was a picture of the gentle, white-haired man who had been in his dream.

In excitement, he rushed into the religious goods store and inquired about the picture and who he was. The man told him it was a picture of Pope Saint Pius X, "our new saint," who was canonized the day before, the day of his dream. He says he knew nothing about Saint Pius X or of the canonization, but again was filled with a sense of deep gratitude and tried to understand the meaning of the dream, especially as it related to his life.

He says he had always had a very special love for the Eucharist, even as a child, years before he could actually receive. He then found out that Pope Saint Pius X was called the "pope of the Eucharist." In part, at least, this is evidently because it was by his influence that the date at which young people could receive their first communion was lowered from adolescence to the present age of six or seven years old.

When he gave us the dream, he reported that the dream had remained with him in almost the same intensity for thirty years. Furthermore, during those years he had realized first a call to be a eucharistic minister as a result of Vatican II and eleven years ago was ordained a permanent deacon in the Roman Catholic church. He sees this ministry as a prophetic one, and it also gives him the privilege of doing communion services. For many years he took communion to the rural poor, especially the old, poor Mexican farm workers who had no one to minister to them. He adds, "There are many deeper meanings of the dream that I experience to this day, but that would be the subject of another paper."

It seems to us that the dream can be seen as a ritual ordination which prefigured his ordination as a permanent deacon twenty years later. It is easy to see that the young man was probably in conflict in 1954. He was obviously devout, as expressed in his custom of going to the cathedral to give thanks at reuniting with his fiancée. He was also obviously drawn to the marriage with his fiancée, who became his wife. It is not hard to imagine that he was at the same time drawn toward a vocation to the priesthood, yet those two "longings of his heart" were incompatible under the rules of his church. In this conflict an image of the Self as a wise priest and saint came to him in his dream, and they "became one." A unity was presented to him, which he could not understand at the moment, and only later when some of the rules changed could he become the eucharistic minister he felt called to be.

To compound this remarkable experience, he reported another "interesting coincidence" that occurred fifteen or twenty years ago:

> A friend of a friend of mine was in Rome, and when he returned to Denver, he called me and told me that while he was in Rome he came across a most appealing wood carved statue that was very beautiful to him, but he did not understand the attraction because he did not know who the carving represented, nor was he a Catholic and never had any appeal or any reverence to statues, saints, et al.
>
> However, on impulse, he purchased it and lugged it all around

Europe with him, took it back on the plane. When he returned to Denver, he did not have any idea why he purchased it, nor did it have any appeal for him any more. So he called me to see if I could tell him who the statue was and to see if I had any interest in it. He said my name just came to him and he phoned me. (Remember, I barely knew this man.)

In the next few days, I drove to his home and was astonished to see this wood carved, hand-painted statue was almost *five feet tall* and even more astonished to see that it is a statue/wood carving of Pope St. Pius X. I could not believe that this person would lug such a big statue all over Europe and even on the airplane with him, but the mystery of my dream was re-opened by his being attracted to it and then thinking of me. I had not told anyone about this dream, except my fiancee.

The statue has been in my closet now for these past fifteen to twenty years. Yes, I purchased it from him, and it was a very small amount of money.

It does not seem to be stretching a point, in view of the times the dreamer reports—getting the statue fifteen to twenty years ago and having the dream's mystery "re-opened," and being ordained eleven years ago—to speculate that this synchronicity was significant in his decision for ordination. The end of this remarkable tale seems best reported in his own words:

Last October while in Rome for the priests and deacons retreat at the Vatican, I had the joy of seeing the remains of Pope St. Pius X in St. Peters. We celebrated mass over his remains in a glass case under an altar in St. Peters. He is dressed in his papal robes, and I know it is he who visited me so many years ago, but still do not fully understand. It was so awesome to see his remains that I cannot even begin to explain, but I know we were one.

# 11

# The Return

When the hero quest has been accomplished—through penetration to the source, or through the grace of some male or female, or animal or divine figure—the adventurer still must return with the treasure, the life-transmuting trophy. To complete the circle, the standard pattern requires that the hero bring home the benefit, whether the Golden Fleece or the sleeping princess or some other prize. The treasure must be brought back into the "kingdom of humanity," where the hard-won victory may benefit and help renew the whole community, or the nation, or all of humankind.

Many fairy tales end at the point of union: they lived happily ever after. The task is complete, and the opposites come together, as when Cinderella marries the prince or Gretel frees Hansel after the witch is burned up. In psychological terms one could say that the ego is redeemed from the symbolic deficiency of the fairy tale curse and moves from a limited, one-sided state to a closer approximation to the Self. As noted, something may be left behind or sacrificed, but often it is not so much sacrificed as transformed. There is an enlargement of personality, which will include the valuable aspects in a new and acceptable form. Yet there is a community significance in the return, as well as an individual.

Joseph Campbell speaks of myth and fairy tales (and dreams) as revealing "the specific dangers and techniques of the dark interior way from tragedy to comedy," the going down and the coming back up "which together constitute the totality of the revelation that is life."[1] One who stays below the threshold, even grasping the treasure which has been won, is staying in the world of tragedy. It is noteworthy that the very titles of Shakespeare's plays, for example, tend to have the names of individuals in tragedies *(Hamlet, Othello, King Lear)* and rather general titles in comedies *(Twelfth Night, A Midsummer Night's Dream, As You Like It)*. In the comedies, and even more in the later romances, people work, change, accomplish tasks, but after it all, they are reincorporated into the group. Whatever they have become is available for the world.

The term *antihero* has been used in discussing contemporary literature to describe a character who stands against the values and customs of society, as a hero often seems to do. The antihero often experiences the same pattern of development which marks the journey of the hero. Something happens which leads or stirs the protagonist, the antihero, to revolt. The threshold of rebellion is crossed and the antihero has departed from the prevailing culture's expectations. Flight from arrest may be necessary, or imprisonment may follow. If the former, ways of avoiding arrest are learned; if the latter, the rules of prison life become a part of the experience.

In Sillitoe's *Loneliness of the Long Distance Runner*,[2] a novel and subsequent film of the early 1960s, the protagonist experiences both—a fleeing from the police and being incarcerated. In both experiences his own value system is strengthened, and he begins to understand what his world view entails. Perhaps he also recognizes, at least more clearly, the faults and shortcomings of the society against which he has rebelled.

Stories of antiheroes tend to leave the tale there, and we suggest that is why the chief protagonist in such a story is seen as an *anti*hero. One could say that the antihero is a hero who has failed to reach the last stage: the return with the treasure. The old society has not changed or come to see the wisdom of the antihero's point of view, so that even at the end of the adventure, the hero is still seen as against society. Or it may be that the antihero still abrogates to him or herself the total power to declare truth—that great danger of hubris. As Jung puts it, "The [transformed personality] has such an immense fascination for the conscious mind that the ego all too easily succumbs to the temptation to *identify* with the hero, thus bringing on a psychic inflation with all its consequences" [italics added].[3]

The basic motifs in the experience of human development and spiritual growth are present in both the stories of heroes and so-called antiheroes. The latter simply stop short of the third stage: bringing that which has been accomplished or learned home to society in general. Actually, though, the antiheroes of the sixties have come to see many of their values accepted by society in general in the seventies and eighties; perhaps they can no longer be considered antiheroes.

The presence of antihero stories may well reflect the difficulty sociological and psychological perspectives seem to have in coming together. Sociologists tend to criticize as "navel gazers" those who talk about the individual's experience of growth and development. The self-actualization people, on the other hand, may get so enraptured with the process that they ignore the final step of the hero journey: the return to society with the treasure. We suspect that too often those concerned with society get impatient with the tasks and lessons to be learned in the second stage.

In the churches one form or expression of this dichotomy is seen in those who emphasize personal religion and those who are social activists. Too often they have little use for each other, whereas if the pattern of spiritual growth and development is properly understood (and the third stage completed) they complement each other.

Our concern is to look at the individual's hero journey. Not everyone will be a culture hero in the larger sense. One's contribution to society as a whole may be small. It may be no more than simply "no longer being a part of the problem." The so-called "hundredth monkey phenomenon" suggests that each individual's accomplishment—such as growth in consciousness—does eventually (when there are enough individuals with that experience) have an impact on society. It is probably in this sense that Joseph Henderson asserts, "The ego as hero is always essentially a bearer of culture rather than a purely egocentric exhibitionist."[4]

When the problem of the return is presented, there is, though, sometimes a refusal of the return. The hero accomplishes something, but stops short. The lesson is incomplete. The hero or antihero is unwilling to share it with others, or the difficulty of the return seems unnecessary or foolish. The psychological development of the hero stops short of its natural completion. The development of a "love for others" has not been achieved or received. It is, to that extent, a *failed* hero journey.

Sometimes there is a "rescue from without." Special aid may be presented to help with the return—perhaps as a result of the relationship achieved with a super power. The final crisis comes, however, with the crossing of the return threshold. The hero is now a *changed person*. She or he is not the same person who set out on the quest. There is now the possibility of confronting the home place with an elixir that can transform society or at least the family.

Perhaps you have known, as we have, wives or husbands who have set out on a journey of spiritual development, worked at it, won through to the treasure, and then tried to bring it home to their spouse. This is a task that has to be done with care! Those who have not been through trials, through the belly of the whale, may not even think what the hero brings home *is* a treasure! The people in the home country may not have enough ego strength to stand an ego-shattering, even though life-redeeming, elixir or "saving truth."

Some will not have, as Jesus called it, "ears to hear." In a way Saint Paul's experience as a Hellenistic Jew, whose life had been transformed by his encounter with the Lord on his way to Damascus, illustrates the difficulty of a return with a treasure. Paul wanted to share the good news that he had found—namely, that there was an answer to the problem of moral failure. God had intervened on behalf of humankind! Paul tried to bring it "home" to the center of his Hellenistic world, Athens. He met with a very cold reception. Paul had to learn other ways of sharing his good news. Yet at least he knew that if the treasure was brought home only to oneself, it was not enough. The completed journey involves a sharing with others.

There is also the danger that the treasure may be misunderstood or not appreciated for what it is. The hero has the problem of communicating the nature of what has been found. Symbols are the bridge between two realities, between different worlds; they provide the connection. As the "master of two worlds" the hero has the problem of sharing a truth that was learned in "another world," from a different perspective. Symbols are the vehicles for that kind of communication.

The symbols must not be taken "concretely" or mistaken for the final term, the transcendent in whose reality they participate. That would be the problem of *idolatry*, which the hero may well encounter on the return when the treasure is presented. Idolatry is taking something less than the "ultimate" and treating it as ultimate. It is making a small concern an ultimate concern. The problem of the theologian, for example, is to *keep the symbol translucent,* so that it may not block out the very light it is supposed to convey. The sacraments in catholic tradition and the Bible in protestant tradition have sometimes had this problem: they have sometimes been taken "only concretely" and not symbolically and so failed to make present the transcendent reality to which they pointed.

Heroes who have won through and made the return are indeed "masters of two worlds." They have been reborn. They are no longer confined or trapped in the values of the society from which they left, even though they continue to live there, but they participate in another world, another truth, another set of values, as well. They have a larger perspective. The goal of the hero journey in its largest or most ultimate sense is to *reconcile* the individual consciousness with the universal, with God, or however the transcendent is conceptualized. In that reconciliation the hero finds a new "freedom to live."

If the treasure is brought home only to one's family, one's tribe, or one's nation, it is only a partial solution to the psychological problem of human development. The individual story must, in some way, be seen to be related to, or a part of, the larger story for it to be meaningful. A "connection" is needed. Most of the world has not self-consciously articulated their view of life and their own life in this way, but we are suggesting that to find life meaningful, one needs to see one's personal story as a part of a larger whole. This is what Jung meant by finding one's own personal "myth of meaning."

The Christian story (and many other stories not specifically Christian) hold up *love* as the ultimate goal for human development. The Creator (who is love) *lures* one along the journey to become more loving. If one wins through to that treasure, then that is the great boon which can be shared on the return home. In the Christian story, the good news is that God has intervened to help overcome the alienation humanity experiences. Part of the meaning of the story of Jesus is that in his life and teaching there are hints about the nature of the human developmental task. There is both the call and the response to the call. Monica Furlong, in discussing Christ as an archetypal image of the Self, says "that reflection of the God-experience in man which makes it possible for him to respond to the call toward wholeness, toward a unifying experience," specifically relates Christ to the hero journey:

Christ is the journeying hero who endures joy and pain, death and rebirth, and the agony of cruxifixion is seen as the deathly experience of conflict faithfully undergone until it yields its unimaginable, and creative result. Christ is the human experience seen in section, as it were, and even if we do not begin to share conventional Christian belief, we may perhaps recognize the similarity of the Christ-experience to states of mind that we have undergone, and which we have seen others undergo.[5]

The story of Jesus and its relationship to the pattern of the hero journey has been well described in more detail in Gerald H. Slusser's *From Jung to Jesus: Myth and Consciousness in the New Testament*.[6]

The Christian story has a third section, as in the pattern of the hero stories. Jesus is indeed "the master of two worlds"; and in the resurrection encounters that follow, a new community is born. There is a transformation, a new birth, a saving truth, that is available to all. Some in the Christian tradition have difficulty recognizing a point that we feel is true; namely, in a culturally pluralistic world to render a story only in its particularity limits its credibility. The recognition of the universal patterns expressed in a story makes the story *more* available to one's personal experience, not less so. Recognition of such universal patterns may bring greater understanding to one's movement through one's own story or journey.

The contribution each individual needs to make as an adult is to complete the journey of development. Having undergone the road of trials and learned the needed lessons, one needs to bring home the treasure of consciousness to one's community or society. Social action is most helpful when it is accomplished by a person who is centered in his or her own wholeness. In a life lived responsibly in this way one has done something for humankind.

This understanding of the return from the hero journey overcomes the conflict some interpreters have raised between the individualism of the hero journey and the concerns of the community. When the return to the community is understood as integral to the completion of the hero journey, the meaning and purpose of each hero's increment of consciousness is seen as significant for the community, as well as for the progress of the individual toward greater wholeness.

The "treasure" is, as we have said, consciousness. The more conscious one is, the more possible it is to show acceptance and true love of others. That is what is brought, in the deepest sense, to the community at the end of the hero journey.

### The Wedding That Never Happened

At a time when she was struggling with a number of paradoxes in her life, one young woman dreamed a return motif (a wedding) for which she was evidently not yet ready:

> We went to a wedding—I was there with Lil and someone else. I didn't really know the bride or groom, but Lil did. The wedding was in a place that looked like a palace. We were sitting and visiting with the bride before the wedding started. She was dressed casually (like wearing jeans). Then when it was time for the ceremony she was very ornately dressed—especially her hair and veil. She had a high veil like a princess would wear.
>
> As they arrived in the big room, the bride's father was ushering them in a horse-drawn carriage. Her father was steering the two horses who started moving faster and faster until he (the father) fell off and landed under the carriage. The horses couldn't be stopped, and they carried the bride and groom off to a distant place where they kept going around in circles. The wedding never happened.
>
> A friend of mine, Nancy (who used to be a sister), was there dressed in habit. She had come from out of town for the wedding. She didn't know the bride or groom either. She was angry that I was with other friends and when I went to say "hi" she was very cold.

The most striking thing about the dream to the dreamer was that the wedding never happened. She understood a wedding to be an integration of some conflict, the coming together of opposites; and the dream indicated, as she put it, that the "union of the paradox is not there yet."

Her two friends in the dream were two people she actually knew, both of them people who needed constantly to be in control, for example, in a possessive way in relationships. She knew that though she appeared outwardly to be a gentle, compliant person, she in fact had a difficult time with her own tendency to be controlling, sometimes on an unconscious level.

When she began to reflect on the paradoxes with which she struggled, there were many. Besides control, she worried about what it meant to try to live simply in the midst of wealth in this country. She worried that the United States, though a "free" country, still had many unfreedoms; what could she do to bring about change? What was her call in the different roles she had—as mother, a person interested in peace work, as wife, as spiritual director for others, as youth minister at her church? In her own uncertainties, it is no wonder there was no resolution in the dream, no living happily ever after.

The dream probably offers her some interesting clues to reflect on the things which work against the resolution of her conflicts. The clothes that are worn in a dream frequently indicate a persona issue—a comment on the dreamer's way of relating to the outer world, on the "me" that is presented to the world. Here even the bride is of two minds about her wedding garment. The shadow-figure bride either wears jeans or dresses like a princess—two extremes that are so far apart as to indicate a tension.

The fact that it is her father who steers the carriage and drives the horses faster and faster may indicate either a pattern of attitudes or behaviors from her personal father or a father-principle-animus set of attitudes driving her libido (the horses) so fast they run away.

Of course, as indicated above, the controlling shadow figures are a clue to look for such behavior in herself, so that she too (like the bride and groom) will not continue "going around in circles." Struggling with these clues and connecting them with her life may help her solve the paradoxes.

### Ripe for the Harvest

The Australian man who worked on his cancer fears in the dream reported in Chapter 6 under the title "An Autopsy" continued to work on dreams after that one. He said they brought him a lot of healing and a tremendous understanding of the difficulties he had experienced, but he wondered "what I had to show for the struggle I endured." Then he had this dream:

> I was at the District where I grew up and Jack, my cousin, and I were looking at this crop. There was 1000 acres of wheat, and it was ready to harvest. The paddock was part of a large property owned by the Williams family. The crop was over ripe and looked to be a very good

crop, but there was one patch that had quite a few weeds through it. We were in a truck with Jack driving, and we were going fairly fast and recklessly around a bush track that surrounded the crop. I wondered why there was no machinery there preparing to harvest the crop.

The Williams family was one he admired. They were wealthy people who had lost their only son as an adolescent. The family then gave away much of their money toward building a hospital.

He thus understood the crop on their land to represent the fruit of his own works, which "comes from land that has known heartbreak, but that pain has been turned into health and healing for others." He thought the dream held out to him the possibility that the crop, which could be the fruit of his labors, "can nourish people physically as wheat can be made into bread and also spiritually as wheat is made into the Bread of Eucharist."

The weeds signified the problems which could be sorted out "at harvest time."

His cousin Jack he saw as fairly cynical and fearful, thus representing the shadow part of him that feared accepting what he had going for him for fear of failure or disaster. He felt that he needed to understand and come to peace with the part of his life that is represented by Jack and "go peacefully and methodically about using the gifts that I have because they are the result of honest labour and have been nurtured and grown to be used for God's purposes."

This seems to be a dream of promise that encourages him to recross the threshold of the return and bring that which he has for the good of the community.

## Sunrise After the Dark

An integrative dream which suggests the time for the return of the hero with her newfound treasures of strength and insight came to a thirty-eight-year-old married woman with children at the end of her therapy. She had entered therapy two years before with a number of serious family and marital problems and had worked personally on healing both current and past wounds. At the beginning of her work she felt trapped, imprisoned by the complexity of the problems. Like many women in traditional relationships, she felt powerless. When she did try to exercise power, she felt guilty. Again like many who feel themselves in this bind, she became manipulative. All this awareness was hard for her to face, but she had accepted this shadow part of herself (which, of course, did not mean that she was always able to act on the knowledge).

She had, however, reached the point where she was recognizing and using her own power in more straightforward, creative ways—even in public forums of social action, such as legislative committee hearings. She had recently been recognized with an award for some of this public work—a far cry from the shy, trapped woman of two years before. During the month after her award, she had this dream:

> I'm walking somewhere in the dark with someone. As we go around the corner of a covered mall, my companion disappears or drops back, and I continue walking alone. Out of the darkness on the left someone is crouching and jumps at me. We wrestle, and I am more powerful and get her arms locked behind her and lift her to a grassy area (like a park) and pull out handcuffs and really secure the hold.
> 
> Then I carry her back through shops as I've come. We weave through a doorway and into a "work-type" shop (industrial arts type) full of men. They stare at us, and we just go through the room and exit out a back door. We're on a landing and go down some stairs into a rough-looking backyard.
> 
> It's still dark. I can't see a gate to get out of the yard, but I can see the yard is full of dogs. As always, I'm afraid of the dogs and can't seem to move off of the stairs.
> 
> Suddenly, to my right side a girl (about 20-ish) appears—she's vague—I can't describe her, yet she almost seems "heavenly," like an angel or spirit form as opposed to human form. She points to a gate, and then I can see it, as well as the layout of the yard. It's rather junky—bare dirt, scraps of grass, garbage cans, lots of dogs, inner-city type, uncared-for yard.
> 
> We start to approach the gate to exit, and I realize the dogs aren't barking or coming near us—just there, watching us leave. We walk a few blocks, and I don't know where to go or where I'm at. It seems I'm lost and don't know where to go, so we turn back.
> 
> My captive/attacker and I seem to be friends now, and she's no longer captive or attacking. We resume walking, seem to be by a nice, green park. Sunrise breaks through the sky. We hop into a car that's just there at the curb—it's a small sports car. I drive and we seem to be going out for breakfast at some restaurant.

Considering the dream's imagery, she commented first on the darkness, which she associated with being unconscious, and on the sense of not knowing where she was going or where she had been. The dream begins with a setting like Dante's *Divine Comedy*—darkness and confusion. That certainly is the way she had been when she began her inner work, and it was still the way she felt much of the time. Yet the dream's movement points to movement in her own life.

In describing the attack of the female figure, she commented, "I'm surprised I could overpower her since I'm so unaware of her existence in my life at a conscious level. I seem to be strong, powerful, and able to handle the situation." The resolution of the conflict within herself is represented by the befriending of the shadow figure, who no longer must be either an attacker or a captive.

She associated the shops with all the "places" she had thought about in her life during the therapy work and the backyard as the unpleasant parts of her life from childhood on, as well as her fears. She had been frightened by dogs for much of her childhood, and an early dream in her therapy work had contained very threatening dog imagery. She wrote, "I'm thrilled about the change in dogs from my first dream long ago with dogs." The friendliness of the dogs symbolizes that she is no longer afraid of all the wounds and threats of her childhood, so that she can now pass through her memories without fear or shame.

The heavenly person is a helper who brings light into the darkness, enabling this change to come about, enabling her to see clearly and without fear all the junky parts of life—and still go on. She points the way to the gate, which has been hidden before. There *is* a way out of all the junk and garbage; she need not remain caught in it.

There is still work to be continued, of course, but she is definitely in a different place in knowing her own strength and being able to handle life. When she realizes that strength and exercises it fearlessly, the dogs neither bark nor come near her. Even more amazing, her captive/attacker is suddenly her friend—no longer captive—she has a car to drive away in, and like an early Hollywood movie, the sunrise breaks through the sky.

She herself saw this imagery as representing the reconciliation of unknown or unconscious parts of herself coming together and of going on with life. She says, "Even though I don't know where to go, I seem to feel good about going. Daybreak and sunrise seem promising, a new beginning." It felt to her like an overview of the work she had done, and even more, it was a strong encouragement that she could recross the threshold of her life after her inner journey into the depths. She could bring this new treasure of strength and awareness back to her family and its problems.

The hero journey is probably seen in its best perspective when one stays aware of those shadow parts which remain, tempting one to stay a victim of the power of old weaknesses, old complexes. Part of the return humility is knowing that one still needs love and patience and consideration, just as part of the return strength is knowing that one has changed and achieved something important.

### The Amazing Air Scooter

The return of the hero is frequently not as spectacular as might be expected; there is seldom a hero's ticker tape parade. It may well be more like the experience the hobbits had at the end of *The Lord of the Rings*.[7] When they got back home after all their adventures and triumphs, there was nobody much who knew anything of their achievement. They even had some more cleansing work to do—to clean out some of the remnants of the evil kingdom from their own home.

This is like most of us when we finish some major task and then just need to go back to our mundane lives, living and working out what our new life will be like now. Accepting one's power and authority, yet not using it badly as one lives each day, is the hero's task. While this is being lived, no one else really knows that one is a hero, which is probably the last and most important part of the task.

One dream spelled this out for the minister of a large urban church on the Monday morning of Holy Week, leading up to Easter:

> Another person, a man friend, and I are flying an air scooter. I'm in control and come to phone wires and try to decide whether to fly over or under. Each time I ask the other man. He usually advises not going under. He says it's better to turn away and just stay low than to try to go under it. Several times I go under the wires and make it, but with a scary feeling.
>
> Finally we land and inspect the machine. I am amazed that such a tiny craft will carry two people through the air.

Holy Week was always a stressful time for him, especially because of all the extra sermons to be prepared, each of which he felt had to be special. The friend with him in the air scooter was someone he actually knew, though not someone he was in current contact with. The friend was an older minister whom he had known for some years, a wise person and a "tremendous preacher." He thus seemed to represent a positive shadow figure, a part of the dreamer of which he was not aware. The presence of this figure was in itself encouraging to the dreamer about his own preaching.

There is a pun acted out in the dream. Each time the dreamer tried, he just barely "made it under the wire." This is the way he usually felt about his own sermon preparations, but when he looked back on the dream after Easter, he realized that, though he had been as anxious as usual at the beginning of Holy Week, he had actually gotten through it this time with a relaxed and easy manner, unlike his usual pattern. It seemed as if this positive shadow figure had been with him during this Holy Week, helping him to "turn away" from his anxiety. Maybe he had been able to "stay low," rather than think of Holy Week as dependent on him. As one of the songs in *My Fair Lady* puts it, "Without your pulling it, the tide comes in."

Deeper work with the dream and with his own "hang-ups" revealed to him that he tended to avoid or resist letting himself be aware that he had achieved something good. He remembered that his mother had always acted as if he were so special that he had come to view himself as inadequate—in reaction to her elevating him so. He felt himself as low and incapable as she had felt him high and special.

It is one of the anomalies of human development that when a child is treated as special by a parent—beyond any realistic assessment—the effect on the child is sometimes negative. The child can end up, as this dreamer did, feeling especially inadequate to the tasks of life. How can this intention of the parent have the opposite effect on the child? When the child's specialness is so exaggerated that the child never feels accurately *seen* as her or his own person by the parent, the child does not learn to value him or herself. When the reflection from the parent is so far from reality, it does not encourage the self-acceptance which parental love can create. Instead, it seems to leave the child with very low self-esteem, as if there is an empty place inside where there should be a secure sense of self-value. In other words, the parent sees a projection, instead of really seeing the child. Something deep within the child senses this idealization, and like all projections, it begins to feel heavy and to undermine the child's sense of personal reality.

This dreamer had an experience in childhood of such an idealized projection, never felt really "seen" by his mother, and thus somehow never felt himself to be acceptable as he was. So he never felt he could really achieve appropriately and was surprised when he was a success. Just as he was surprised when he achieved success, the dream shows him amazed that this tiny "craft" could carry him through the air—amazed that with the craft he could fly. When he "came down to earth" after Holy Week, he could experience this same sense of amazement.

Not only was the dream a turning point in his enjoyment of Holy Week, but in subsequent months it also seemed to mark a turning point in his beginning to be able to appreciate and live out his own skill and craft as a minister. He saw that he had achieved many things in life and that he was no longer the little boy who needed to be embarrassed by his mother's pushing him forward as special. He could live his life without this anxiety, enjoying his vocation on a daily basis without need for either grandiosity or self-abasement. He had brought his treasure home.

## Danger of Becoming What We Hate

At the time of the next dream (one of Jean's), she had worked hard for over two years meeting the requirements for the level of certification called "diplomate" in the American Association of Pastoral Counselors (AAPC), her professional society. This designation, among other things, is the credential which allows her to supervise other pastors and pastoral counselors in their counseling work. With it the diplomate is certified as a trainer and teacher of others.

One of the requirements (or, as those working on it are inclined to say, "one of the hoops to be jumped through") is the composition of a paper explaining one's theory of supervision, demonstrating the supervisor's personal understanding of what needs to be learned and how that learning can best be facilitated. Jean worked *obsessively* on the draft of the paper night and day the last weekend before she needed to mail it to her supervisor for his suggestions. The day after she mailed the draft of the paper, she had a frightening dream:

> There was a young man who was palling around with a group of guys. The evil leader then said to two of them that it was time to bring him "fully" into the group. This meant they were going to torture him horribly till he was bleeding and beaten down. The idea of this torture was that he then could become a torturer like they were. The last scene of the dream was a picture of him on the floor of a cave, broken and bloody.

In the tasks in which she was currently engaged, Jean did feel tortured by all that was needed to bring her "fully" into the group—the AAPC. The tasks of the journey frequently feel like that, and then dreams speak of torture, mutilation, and even death.

Even more, the dream called to her attention her one-sided, neurotic behavior in the obsessive way in which she was going at her work. She needed to be aware that there was an evil leader inside her who was driving her to the night-and-day focus with no rest.

She also saw the dream as a warning not to become a torturer in the way she herself gave training and supervision to others. The dream clearly shows that one who has experienced torture may in turn become a torturer, and human history is full of examples. There is even a way in which, the dream suggests, the group itself may become addicted to the idea that torture is the way to behave. As a member of the group, the boy in the dream was expected by the others to become a torturer.

As Jean moved toward the "highest" designation in the AAPC, she was facing the danger of hubris, just as had the dreamer in the shark dream in Chapter 16 after her first workshop, and just as had the counselor who dreamed of the whip-snapping cowboy in the western saloon in Chapter 9. Once one works up the courage to accept one's authority, the opposite danger comes into play—the danger of overidentifying with the power. If she stays in a kind of proud enjoyment of her status, she too can become a torturer.

As Jean came to understand this part of the dream's meaning, it warned against the danger of identifying with the process as she experienced it. ("I had to go through this hard work, so everyone else must go through it too.") The process must never become mere hazing, but on the other hand, it must maintain the integrity of good standards, even if the requirements cause pain in the learning.

For example, the writing of the paper about her theory of supervision had been a torture to Jean, yet her own pain could not be the sole touchstone of what she thought was good and needed in the training of counselors and supervisors. Pain in the context of the hero journey is neither good nor bad in itself. The questions to be asked are: did this requirement teach what I needed to know? Did it help me grow? Did it help me spot bad habits and slough them off, blind spots and bring them to light?

Thoughtful answers to such questions, shared with others in a mutual sorting process, can be a treasure for the whole community as well as the individual on the journey. In the dream, the young man ended beaten and bloody on the floor of the cave, with the *idea* on the part of the others that he in turn could become a torturer like them; but he does not have to do so. The dream thus ends with open possibilities.

As a part of unraveling this meaning of her torture dream, Jean came to see that, as hard as the paper on supervision was for her to write, it had probably been the most valuable part of her own training in supervision. Probably in part because she operates on the intuitive, feeling levels of psychological type, the careful, ordered understanding of the processes she uses do not come to her easily. The requirement that she study and objectify the process and her own values changed the way she did supervision for the better. Without the writing of the paper as a tortuous task, she would not have done that needed part of her own development, and therefore would have been less useful for the community of pastoral counselors.

By showing her these horrible outcomes, the dream helped give her the energy to avoid them (or so she hopes). Thus, the psychic snapshot of what she was doing to herself on the obsessive surface level enabled her to sort out what choices she wanted to make on a number of different levels. Work with the torture dream during her road of trials came to point the way to an appropriate return she can try to make, a road sign pointing the way across the return threshold.

The question always remains: can the hero return with the treasure? Can the hero continue to work out in daily living the new insights, consciousness, and strengths which have come to pass during the journey? If so, the community as well as the hero is enriched. If not, perhaps another call to adventure will come around and the hero will have another chance.

# Part III
# Dream Series

*What we call the beginning is often the end
And to make an end is to make a beginning.
The end is where we start from. . . .*

*We shall not cease from exploration
And the end of all our exploring
Will be to arrive where we started
And know the place for the first time.*

*T. S. Eliot*

# ▶12

# Dreams and Suicide

In this chapter we present a series of terrifying dreams, which we will not interpret fully because of their complexity. Yet the sense of impending trouble is very clear, as well as the seriousness of the dangers to the dreamer, whom we will call Kay. The first four dreams occurred, as she put it, in "Advent of 1979," all within an eight-day period. At the time she was forty-six years old, married, with two adult daughters, one in college and one working. She herself worked as a telephone operator. The minister of her church was her spiritual director, and she felt better about working with him than with other people who had tried to help her with inner healing.

She recorded the first dream in her journal, but did no further work with it:

> I am in a big, old house standing by an upstairs window. There are sheer curtains at the window, and I move one aside to look out over the lawn and trees toward the lake. Out on the lake is a small boat. My husband is in it. He is fishing.
> 
> And then a bee flies in through the window and stings me, and I see demonic faces around me, laughing and saying, "That's what you get for spying!" I protest that I'm not spying, and it was only a bee-sting. But they continue laughing and say, "But you will die, die, die." I feel the swelling start in my throat—I can't swallow, I can't breathe—I can't cry out.

There are very few clues here except the frightening tone of the dream. Kay is in an "old house," indicating perhaps an old set of attitudes or behaviors that she "lives in." Her husband is in contact with the water, fishing in a boat, perhaps suggesting fishing up something out of the depths of the unconscious. The danger to her is also clear, but her only association with the meaning of the motif of "spying" was the feeling that she had no right to be where she was—that something about "where she was" was wrong.

Traditionally, bees are associated with diligence, creative activity, and even wealth, evidently because of their busy activity and production of sweet honey. They are hard workers. For some reason, perhaps because they can fly and transcend earth, they are associated in several cultures with the soul, with immortality and rebirth, with order and purity. Being bitten by something suggests being presented with whatever it symbolically represents. Thus, Kay had been "stung" by all that the bee symbolizes, and she feared that she could not swallow, breathe, or speak because of the bee sting. The new "sting" was terrifying to her.

The second dream is also frightening:

> I was walking, not knowing where to go, but soon found myself walking along the banks of a seashore. They are covered with tall, rather brown grass bending in the breeze. There is a path along the top of the bank and a bench that overlooks the sea. I sit on the bench and watch the gulls soaring, feel the sun on my face, smell the sea.
>
> Then I notice a figure down on the beach among the rocks. It is my husband and he calls to me to come down to see the shells he has found—and I don't want to go. I'd rather not be outdoors anyway, but I am—and I am content on my bench. It is peaceful. But he is insistent.
>
> I look up the shore, and I see a dust storm or sand storm coming with great swiftness. I call out to him and start running down the embankment. The wind whips the grasses against my legs. They cut. The sand is swirling around and I cannot breathe, but I must get to him. I call out—Jesus, help me—but he does not appear, although I get down to the beach and the storm is stilled.
>
> And Roger is buried by the sand—there is one hand sticking out. I tell myself that I should be digging him out—but I don't. I reach down and take his hand instead, and as I hold it, I seem to become black, dripping, and bloody. It is as if I am melting, I am becoming less and less—a bloody, tarry pool on the beach.

Several of the motifs from the first dream are repeated in the second: there is the water and the shore, her husband is closer to the water than she, she is contented to stay where she is (especially if she is somewhat hidden), she cannot breathe, and she is threatened with a nameless kind of destruction.

After the second dream, she recorded in a journal that this might be saying something about her marriage relationship and how discontented and smothered (unable to breathe) she felt. She adds, "I was also fearful that if I stayed as I was that I would simply not be."

Both of the dreams use spiritual imagery—the demonic faces in the first dream and her calling on Jesus for help in the second (after which the storm is stilled). In the second dream there is also more action on her part—more of a sense that she could do something about the situation. She runs toward her husband when she sees the storm coming, and she tells herself she should be digging him out of the sand. She seems to have some choices; but when she does not exercise the choice to dig him out, she becomes a bloody, tarry pool.

With hindsight some years later, she no longer thought the dream was about her marriage, though there had been problems in the relationship. She later realized that she blamed the marriage for whatever was wrong with her life because that would have been easier to work on than to face her inner work—easier than to face her inner animus. She was terrified to move forward to something she was being called to face. In fact, when she takes no action toward digging out her husband (and whatever he represents in the dream), she melts away, becomes "less and less," and nothing is left of her except a "bloody, tarry" mess. She will simply cease to exist, in the demanding language of the dream, unless she begins to act.

The third dream has another storm and brings in the motif of death and mutilation:

> I am in the midst of a large meadow or field. The sun is shining; the breeze is blowing softly. There is nothing to be seen in any direction but more tall grass—no trees, nothing else. But as I am looking, something dark appears on the horizon. As it gets larger I can see that it is a cloud—a storm is coming. The sky darkens, lightning flashes, and it starts to rain. I love the rain and I lift my face eagerly to it.
>
> It continues to come down harder. My clothes are plastered against me and it is cold. The rain begins to hurt, I need shelter, but there is

none. Not even a tree. I think of calling for Jesus, but it doesn't feel right, and I don't do it. The rain has beaten me to my knees—the tall grass is flattening and the ground is muddy and the rain comes harder and harder and I fall on my face in the mud and die.

And the clouds move off and the sun comes out—and magpies appear with it. They peck at my flesh till it is torn and bloody and one takes out my eye and with it in his beak flies toward the sun.

She wrote, "Even though I knew I should work with the symbols, I began to be caught up in the idea that my dreams were telling me to commit suicide. I began to plan how." This is a clear and interesting example of two dangers in dream work: taking dream symbols concretely instead of symbolically (even though she sensed the symbols were important) and thinking that any dream *tells one what to do*. Dreams point up the consequences of behavior and choices one makes, but the conscious point of view must always be maintained.

Again there is a water motif, this time in the form of rain, which she first enjoys and then is beaten down by. There is no hiding place from the rain. She is first beaten to her knees, which may be significant after her declining to call on Jesus for help, and then beaten face down into the mud and death. A serious storm is truly upon her, and she is not coping with it.

The specific form of the mutilation is interesting. The birds (spiritual beings, who can transcend earth) peck at her flesh—finally taking out her eye and flying toward the sun with it. Is she supposed to *see* something she is refusing to see? With Jungian understanding of animus symbols as calling us to deeper connections with the Self, as well as the imagery of the birds taking her eye toward the sun, it sounds as though some development in herself is the task toward which she is being called—or perhaps not so much called as browbeaten. Such forceful and terrible dreams usually come when one has ignored milder and gentler nudges, as if to get one's attention by their very horror.

The fourth of the dreams finally got her attention enough to call forth some action on her part:

> I am in a desert at the foot of a large pyramid and someone or something is telling me to climb it. But I don't want to, for I have a deathly fear of snakes and am sure that there will be some on the pyramid sunning.

And then I see steps leading down to what looks like an entrance into the pyramid. I decide to go that way and I find myself in a long dark passageway leading in. I have a lantern which casts flickering light along the walls. There is an ancient "feel" about the place and I reach out and brush my fingers along the wall. The passageway gets narrower and smaller and I come to a small opening like a crevice between rocks. I stoop down and squeeze my way through and find myself in a large chamber.

It is dark but for my lantern—but the air is fresh. I start to look around and I see a bed of snakes in the corner. I am petrified and unable to move as they come toward me. They are surrounding me and a large one in front of me raises itself up to strike. I scream, "Jesus," and I am surrounded by light and the snakes move back except for the one in front of me. And I see that the light in front of me is an angel with a gleaming sword—and looking up I see a shaft out of the chamber.

I don't know how I get up there but I am crawling along it and it is dark and then it ends. It is not a way out. I can see nothing. I press against the end of the shaft. There is no opening. There is nothing but darkness. The only way out is to go back down into the chamber where the very floor undulates as if it were the back of a giant serpent. I press into the darkness. I will not go back down there—I press further into the darkness until I begin to dissolve into it.

As we discussed in the chapter on snakes in our previous dream book, snakes are very complex symbols. Jung says they usually occur when the conscious mind is deviating from its instinctual basis and that they are a well-substantiated archetype of transformation and renewal. The suspicions we have suggested about the three previous dreams—that Kay has some inner work of transformation to do—are thus made specific in this one. However, added to the universal fear of new awareness and challenge which is so often portrayed in snake dreams is Kay's personal association with snakes. She had a genuine snake phobia, reflected in the dream in her reluctance to climb the pyramid for fear she might encounter snakes. Of course, as so often happens when one runs away, the place where she ran to hide was the very place where she encountered that which she most feared.

The snakes thus suggest that Kay is being faced with the challenge to integrate her instinctual base with some new level of consciousness. At the beginning of her dream in the desert (a picture of the dry, arid place she found herself in at the time) she tries to hide, as she had in the other dreams. Her descent into the dark passageway is typical of the dark journeys that can precede some new birth; she is in the spiritual birth canal. She had some light—some consciousness—but the lantern seems small in the vast depths of the ancient pyramid.

There her worst fears come upon her when she spies the bed of snakes. Yet—again a repeated motif from other dreams—she calls upon the name of Jesus, and this time help appears at once: light, the snakes moving back, and an angel with a gleaming sword. This striking image is reminiscent of two biblical stories. The first, which comes as Adam and Eve are banished from the Garden of Eden:

> Then the Lord God said, "Behold, the man has become like one of us, knowing good and evil; and now, lest he put forth his hand and take also of the tree of life, and eat, and live for ever"—therefore the Lord God sent him forth from the garden of Eden, to till the ground from which he was taken. He drove out the man; and at the east of the garden of Eden he placed the cherubim, and a flaming sword which turned every way, to guard the way to the tree of life.[1]

Is Kay being banished from some Garden of Eden where she tries to hide from the knowledge of good and evil? Even more cogent, perhaps, to Kay's situation is the biblical story of Balaam and his ass. Balaam, not seeing what his ass sees all along, continues to beat the animal because it will not go forward. When Balaam's eyes are "opened," he too sees the angel of the Lord standing in the way, with his drawn sword in his hand.[2] Kay laughingly asserted, reflecting on the dream years later, that the story of Balaam not seeing what his ass saw fit her pretty well at the time.

Even though the angel with the sword and the surrounding light protect Kay from the other snakes, she is still confronted by the large one in front of her, raised as if to strike. Again she runs away and tries to hide, but there is no way out. She will not go back to the snakes, but when she presses farther into the darkness, she begins to dissolve—again the warning motif of ceasing to be. It is repeated in the dreams in such varied forms as not being able to speak, dissolving into a bloody, tarry pool, and being beaten down into the mud to die.

Kay felt frightened after this dream and knew she needed some help. She was still concerned that she would choose the option of suicide, but she understood from this last dream that it was not her physical life that was in jeopardy as much as her essential being. She was beginning to avoid the tendency to concretize the dream symbols and to grasp their deeper symbolic significance.

She took these dreams to her spiritual director. After he read them he told her that it seemed she needed more help than he knew how to give her. He asked her permission to refer her to a psychotherapist. She resisted, but when he pointed out that he thought it was essential, she agreed.

She was in therapy for about a hundred hours over a period of a year and was convinced that she "had everything figured out and all together" and was thinking of terminating her counseling. At that point, evidently in an unconscious way, she became angry at her therapist. She wrote of what happened then: "On Thursday I killed myself. It was a voice from outside myself that told me to do this (I know what that sounds like!) and I just gave up and did."

She was clinically dead, but resuscitated in the emergency room. She wrote that when she woke up, she "was psychologically naked—no defenses, no masks. There was really no choice but to face the terror within." The therapy was intensified, and as she says, "I worked!" She had to face her alcoholism, rejection, incest, unworth, and "all the things that people must face." She looked at her rage, lust, and desires to hurt people. She kept a journal with many dark images and fears. She said she really did fear "that if I made this journey to the center that there would be nothing there. I would not exist." From this poignant statement, we can see the conscious fear which the imagery of dissolving reflected in the dreams. This is a powerful example of the terror a reluctant pilgrim can feel at the prospect of going on the hero journey.

Her spiritual director walked this journey with her as far as he was able. He, she, and her therapist met several times, for all of them found it obvious that her psychological journey could not be separated from her spiritual one. About six months before terminating her therapy, two years after the previous four dreams, she had a dream about James, her spiritual director:

> I was at church, in the parish hall. It was between services and James had just been found dead in the church. I was numb and I

lamented the fact that I hadn't gone to the earlier service for I would never hear him preach again. I wondered if I might take his sermon as a keepsake. When he was found there was a book with him that he had marked—it was a book catalog and he had marked several books that he wanted to order. I had that.

But it was time for Eucharist and I went into the church—it was crowded and I wanted to sit up front. I found a place. There was a chalkboard off to one side that he had been writing on when he died. It was somewhat smeared from his arm brushing down it as he fell. It said, "let us live for him, let us play for him"—and then I couldn't stop the tears. The sense of loss was overwhelming and I woke myself.

She understood the dream to say that she could now let go of her dependency on her spiritual director. She had to go on, but now she had the skills and tools to do so. She saw the catalog with the marked books as indicative that she was to continue with her studying and learning. She interpreted the message on the board literally, with the "him" meaning God. This was a reaffirmation of the call she had known in her heart all her life to serve God—not telling her how to go about it, but only pointing the direction. The only clues she got from this dream were that her God was a God of life and play—the message she carried with her from her spiritual director's "last words."

During her therapy she had gone back to college and was near earning her B.A. She earned it *summa cum laude* and was very proud of her accomplishment, even though her mother asked her what she was going to do when she grew up. She saw that even though she knew she would never be able to please her mother, she would probably always fall into the trap of hoping for her approval.

She subsequently earned her M.A. and at the time of this writing was working on a Master of Divinity degree. She feels called to the ordained ministry, but says she will survive if the church says no to that. She and James shifted their relationship to that of close friends and colleagues. She and her therapist write to each other once in a while, and he rejoices in her path. She says her marriage is healthier than it has ever been.

She describes herself this way: "I do not have all my work done. I am not whole, but I continue to grow toward it. Suicide is no longer an option or a threat. I have some skills, I have some tools, I have some friends, and most of all I have a grateful heart."

This is a good description of someone who completed a perilous hero journey and returned with the treasure—just to live life in ordinary, fulfilling ways. By her courageous choices she had made the journey, but at every step of the way she was forced to give up things. All five of these dreams concern something she was losing: staying in the old house, on the bench, or the peaceful meadow, avoiding the snakes of new awareness, and even staying dependent on her beloved spiritual director. All of these were losses which saddened or frightened her. Yet her gains, as she saw clearly years later, were far beyond the losses. Even the loss of her relationship with James was balanced by the gain of a close friend and colleague. The person she had become in her journey was worth the sacrifices.

# ▶13
# A Repeated Symbol

Sometimes on the way along a journey, one dream symbol carries the theme of the dreamer's life over a long period—not that the same precise dream is repeated (though that too may occur), but rather that dreams ring the changes on the same symbol in different settings and stories. Such a series came over a period of several years to a capable woman we will call Nell. The symbol was water—one usually associated with the unconscious.

Since we first began to study depth psychology, we have chuckled over an ambivalent treatment of symbols we noted by experts in the field. They solemnly assure you that dream symbols have *no* absolute meanings; then you tell them a dream, and they begin to tell you that symbol's absolute meaning! Actually, as we have come to discover, there are some symbols which have a continuing meaning because of their very nature.

As we suggested in Chapter 5, the dreamer's personal amplification of dream symbols is of the first importance in interpreting her or his dreams, but there can also be significance in the motifs from general amplification. With such symbols as water, for example, the nature of water can be observed generally. Water is a part of common human experience; life on the planet would be impossible without it. One can see part of the way into water—more deeply if it is still—but not all the way into its depths. Water is filled with life in its natural state; in fact, all of us entered the world by way of water. We drink it, we cleanse ourselves with it, we obtain food from it. In all these aspects it bears a strong connection with the unconscious, and thus is customarily connected with the unconscious.

Nell had a series of water dreams, almost as if once the psyche saw she connected them with the unconscious, it said, "Now then, she will understand water dreams; water dreams she will get." She was a forty-two-year-old woman when she entered therapy because of heavy work pressure and periodic depression, which she hid from co-workers and friends. She reported great difficulty saying no to requests from others and a habit of working even when she took a "day off." People viewed her as responsible (overresponsible?) and competent; she was the support of many people. She was puzzled and angry over her failure to be able to control her feelings, and all of this together made her decide to seek counseling help.

About four months later, after exploring some of her patterns of behavior with the therapist, she dreamed:

> I enter a large auditorium. A woman is teaching using a slide presentation. Carol comes along. I end up holding her, as she is sad and miserable. She calms down. She has a resume ready as she is looking for a new job. We meet some people on the way out who have job offers, and it reminds me that I must prepare to publish for Carol's job opening.
> I am in New Zealand and on the ocean. My Mother is there too with friends. A group of us are walking and must cross a very precarious narrow bridge over the water. It is extremely dangerous. Two persons fall in but we make it.

Nell's associations with the dream described Carol as a person at her office with whom she was secretly very angry because Carol's personal life "intruded" into her functioning at the office. Nell herself *never* allowed her personal life to intrude during office hours.

In the dream, even in the midst of the busy group, Nell realizes how sad and miserable Carol is and holds her, upon which Carol grows calm. It seems reasonable to suppose that Carol is a shadow figure, a part of the dreamer herself, and that she needs to treat herself the way she treated Carol in the dream. She needs to experience her own needs and feelings, instead of being angry at herself because she sometimes becomes depressed. She might be a good deal better off if she sometimes let her personal life "intrude" into the office. By always being so "strong" and having her life so compartmentalized, she treats her depression as if it were the villain instead of realizing her own true needs. Why does she engage in such illogical attitudes? Work with the dream points her toward this way of examining herself and her current depression.

The second half of the dream suggests some clues as to why she behaves so illogically. It also gives some indication that she is beginning to move forward. Her associations with New Zealand were: someplace that is distant, far away—"what I don't know about." Probably one reason she can't understand her own attitudes is that they are so buried in the "ocean" of her unconscious and, thus, far from being known to her. Another clue to the source of her attitudes—a tenuous one at this point—is the presence of her mother. Is the mother part of the source of her attitudes? If so, she may need to investigate what these attitudes are and how her mother lived them and taught them to the dreamer, her daughter.

The prognosis at the end of the dream is of success; though it is "extremely dangerous" and some fall in the water, "we make it." This dream imagery shows the kind of fear, precariousness, and danger with which people approach making changes in their lives and attitudes. This is thus an example of how difficult it is to cross the threshold of a new part of the heroic journey.

In this case, subsequent dreams carried the water imagery on. A month later, she dreamed:

> I am on a large ship. Beth and Nan are there. In order to leave the ship we must walk through the water—it does not appear to be over our heads. When I leave the ship the water level is down. I walk across with a man I am with, but whom I don't recognize. Beth is on the other side and is ill in bed. We walk by her.

The dreamer's two friends, Beth and Nan, are both described by her as strong personalities and both are *very serious*. All three of them need to "walk through the water"—go on an inward journey; and the dream says this will not be so scary as the water seemed in her first dream—it was not "over our heads." The suggestion is also made at the end of the dream that one of her friends, Beth, though described by the dreamer as strong and serious, is ill. Perhaps being strong and serious has something to do with being ill. As suggested before, Nell herself may well be overly conscientious, so that her own needs are neglected by her being too one-sided.

In addition to the two known shadow figures, she encounters an unknown character, a man she walks across with. In a woman's dreams, as we have said, such an anonymous helping man represents an unknown helping part of herself.

Then in another month, just before leaving to spend Christmas with her family, she dreamed:

> I am wading in a lake where people are swimming. I see a body of a boy at the bottom who I am sure has drowned. I pull the body onto the shore and push on his chest, but he does not stir. His younger brother, whom he was babysitting, comes running up. He starts to cry. Meanwhile others come over to us. The drowned boy begins to stir and breathe again to my amazement.

The drowned boy shows how neglected some part of her is—she has let it become drowned in the lake and at first cannot revive it. Whatever this unknown masculine part of herself is, there is danger of losing it. The dream ends amazingly, however, as if to say that all is not lost if she will pay attention to the danger.

With hindsight it is tempting to say that this dream warned Nell to stay aware of the family interactions over her Christmas holiday visit. At any rate, she did watch them and faced for the first time the fact that her mother was insensitive to her, clearly valuing the other children in the family more than she did Nell. Her mother never praised any of her accomplishments, nor, indeed, seemed to value them at all. Her own hard work, then, could be seen as the continuing effort to win her mother's approval.

Nell also realized that she was seldom able to accept compliments from anyone—tending instead to push them away and discount them. When she received a compliment, instead of relaxing and enjoying it, she tended to run all the harder. She then saw that she had "put on" her mother's attitude toward her, as if she were not as good as others. This was a clear connection to her first dream; this was at least part of the attitude of her mother which must fearfully be faced down if she is to get to a new place in her own life, across the narrow, precarious bridge over her own troubled waters.

While she was at home over the Christmas holiday, Nell had two other dreams in which the ocean appears. In one scene:

> On my way back to the car I have to crawl along the rocks back to the car along the ocean. The waves are rushing in and I am afraid of getting water on my camera.

The dream makes the humorous, though nonetheless dangerous, suggestion that the film in her camera may get ruined. She has been "taking pictures" of her family, that is, getting a clear picture of the family interaction. Even when you have begun to see and understand the patterns which go into making you behave as you do, you can still get caught up in them again—particularly when you are again in the presence of those who helped form the pattern. You may have to go back to "crawling" again to maintain your new insights and not let them get lost in the unconscious.

On Christmas morning Nell had a dream which picked up several of these themes:

> I am watching a trip across the ocean—observing deep sea animals. I see whales, alligators, large fish. It is as if I am on a boat going fast across the water or seeing a film of this view. Later I am sitting with a group of persons who study the ocean. They are talking in scientific terms of their trip. A mother brings her daughter who is able to join the group as part of her studies. Those in the group that I recall are men. One stands out as particularly gentle. He is the leader of the group and a priest who lives nearby.

This is a rich dream, showing her on a safe ship, yet in contact with the great ocean. This great ocean-unconscious is being studied by a group of scientists—objective, interested observers; she is not being threatened with drowning, as in her other dreams. The ocean-unconscious contains a rich variety of inhabitants—some dangerous, as the unconscious of all of us does. Nell is one of the calm, objective examiners. Maybe the mother and daughter who join the group are even a symbol of how she might "mother" the "daughter" she is herself—and even get credit for it as part of her studies!

The gentle leader-priest is becoming more visible to her; he is a positive masculine image who can help and lead her.

One incident during the Christmas holiday may connect to the positive imagery in this dream. On one occasion, after Nell had begun to realize her mother's insensitivity, her mother commented after hearing of some accomplishment of another family, "Why don't any of *my* children ever do anything like that?" Feeling stronger than usual and seeing how inappropriate her mother's devaluing was, Nell responded assertively, "I do!" This was a new ability for her, and it may be symbolically portrayed in the dream as the objective scientists and the gentle minister.

The dreams that followed for the next few months carried on this imagery of water and her relation to it. For example, a part of a January dream went as follows:

> My brother and I later must swim to another ship. We board the ship; others are there also. I spend all the time on the ship looking for an object to use as a life preserver, something that will float. I examine pillows and cushions. I am aware that I will be on the water a long time and might not make it. I say good-bye to my parents and thank them. My mother in the dream does not look like my real mother.

This is hardly a joyous return from the journey! In fact, the dream specifically warns her that she will be "on the water a long time and might not make it." The parents in the dream, at least the mother, do not seem to be her outer parents, but perhaps some inner parenting or an "internalized" mother who can be more supportive and affirming than her own mother. The dream clearly indicates it will take a long time to change such a deeply ingrained pattern, and she needs something to help her preserve the "life" in her as she makes the journey to another way of floating on the water—another ship.

While this inner self-examination was going on, Nell was repeating other old patterns at work—not saying no when she needed to, feeling constant pressure to work ever harder, and holding all her anger in. She fretted over whether she should leave her job, but feared that she usually ran away instead of having the courage to face people with the hard things she needed to say. As she worked through this, she decided that whether she left or stayed was less important than whether she herself changed. In support of her effort to live a more humane life, she confronted her boss face-to-face with information on how disregarded she felt. She felt more at ease afterward and subsequently had a peaceful water dream, which she described in part:

> I had been swimming in the ocean in the day and we returned later. The sky was very grey and dark. The waves rolled in gently. We were

able to walk out for a way. There were people walking through the water to the shore. I assisted them.

The water symbolism of Nell's dreams responded quickly to whatever small or large action she was able to take in outer life. In part from such encouragement as this last dream, she decided that even such confrontation with her boss as she could manage was still not enough. The office was not going to change its patterns, and confronting their policies and making a few changes was not enough. She could leave the field of battle with honor and look for a job where she could live a life more consonant with her own value system. She really did not have to keep proving herself through long, demanding hours of constant achievement.

She therefore left her job and took another one (after taking a vacation!) where a more humane, leisurely atmosphere prevailed. She felt she had a clear bead on the inner work she must do to change the old, destructive patterns from her childhood. With her "eternal analyst within" to help her, she could now process her own experiences without the help of her counselor, so she left therapy and settled down to life.

Two years later, however, she began to feel very depressed again and could not get a handle on why she felt that way. As if on cue, she had another ocean dream—her first since the earlier ones. She was swept with despair, thinking she might be "right back where she was before." Here is the dream:

> I am staying at a hotel near the ocean and we are preparing to go into the ocean to see diving whales. We walk along and can see the whales in the distance. We are dressed warmly in anticipation of cold water. My brother Ken is a young boy and I lift him up to see the whales coming out and diving into the water.
> 
> Many people are hiding in a house in the Mid-East like Libya. I sleep and when someone comes I hide under the covers so as not to be recognized.

Her unreasoning fears because of having "another ocean dream" were fed by her sense of unfulfillment in her job. It simply did not have the interest for her nor the scope for her talents that she needed. She had gone from one extreme of a job so demanding that there was no time or energy for anything except her job to the other extreme of a job so undemanding as to be boring. In addition, she had suffered a number of losses of friends, and she had tended to try to suppress how much these hurt (much as she had as a child suppressed how much it hurt not to be affirmed for who she was).

When she examined this dream more thoughtfully, she could see that it was different from the earlier ones. The whales, the great mammals of the ocean, which were also in the positive dream on Christmas, may represent her own inner parenting possibilities. Also, she is not in danger of drowning in the ocean, as she was in some of the earlier dreams, but instead she is taking one of her favorite brothers to see the whales. They are dressed warmly and will be looking at one of the most exciting sights nature holds—these huge mammals who can dive in and come out of the water safely. All this is positive, and Ken probably represents that new masculine part of herself which needs to look at life with objectivity.

There is a warning, though, in the last paragraph, which seems to connect with her feelings of depression. Libya, in her associations, is a very dangerous place, "an unstable, crazy place." This probably connects to the fact that she had been neglecting her connection with her own inner pain, especially over the serious losses in her life; she has been hiding under the covers. The warning is that when she hides from her own pain and too easily puts on a "happy face," she is in a dangerous, crazy, unstable place. The contrast can be seen easily in the first two paragraphs of her dream. In the first she is dressed warmly, watching with Ken from the safe shore. In the second she is cowering under the covers in fear.

The psyche had produced another water dream as if to shock her into remembering what was necessary for her life to be creative. An analyst in Zurich told us of a session when she went in to see Dr. Jung in a very discouraged mood. She was discouraged, she told him, "because I *always* fall into the very same chasm—every time!"

Dr. Jung replied, "Well, yes, you do always fall into the same chasm. That is true. But, you know, I believe that every time you fall in, there is a little more dirt under you." He held up his fingers to estimate about two inches "more dirt."

That story has comforted us. The path is slow, and sometimes one despairs, as Nell did, because of so much work done to change—and then, still, the same chasm. Jung's gesture recognizes the slow nature of human growth and change, but nevertheless asserts the value of such change. It *is* better to have a little more dirt under you each time, and the positive first part of Nell's dream affirms that she has indeed brought home some treasure from her journey into her family depths, even while it warns her that she cannot hide from pain and continuing growth.

# 14

# A Monk's Dreams

Two wonderful dreams, rich in universal religious symbolism, came to a young Christian monk. The heroic motifs are apparent, and his own associations relate them to the inner spiritual journey in which he was engaged. He called the first one "The Three Dragons and the Monkey Prince," and it shows that dragons are alive and well in the psyches of people even today. Here is the dream:

> I was standing on the edge of a great high cliff. It was evening. The landscape is dreary and desolate. Old smoldering stumps of trees can be seen here and there. Everything is charred as though a bomb had recently been dropped on the area. A very dense fog begins to roll in. It becomes more and more foggy until I can see nothing but the grey haze of the fog. I remember how sheer the drop-off is of the cliff on which I am standing and I begin to fear that if I move I may fall—so I stand very still. Suddenly in the midst of the fog I perceive some movement. At first I cannot tell what it is but gradually I begin to realize that in the middle of the sky—level with where I am standing on the cliff—there are three huge dragons wrestling around. Through the fog I just barely catch some glimpses of the thrashing dragon bodies gnarled together in combat. Smoke coming from the dragons smells bad, and I am afraid as I watch the scene.
>
> Then in the middle of the dragon fight, I begin to see a faint orange/red light. It glows softly and seems to become more clear. Out of the light comes some small orange thing—flying in circles. I eventually make out the form and see that it is a little monkey in an orange

Japanese kimono, and he is floating on a feather—a peacock feather, to be exact. He comes flying out of the midst of the battle with his small chest bravely puffed out. He is a monkey, but he has almost a human bearing. He lands at my feet and smiles at me. As he smiles his face changes and becomes almost human. He now has a gold crown on his head, and I think of him as a prince of some kind. Laughing nonchalantly, he takes the crown off his head and, almost unconcerned, throws the little gold crown at the fighting dragons. The dragons disappear in a puff of smoke, the sun comes out on a changed, green and pleasant landscape, and the little monkey prince looks at me laughing as if it is all a great joke.

The dreamer shared with us in a letter his "explanation of my understanding of dream" as follows:

You told me to write a brief note of explanation concerning my understanding of one meaning of this particular dream.

At the time I had this dream I was in a time of great inner struggle. I became painfully aware of the power of three rather "primitive" and instinctual energies within that I felt somewhat helpless before (i.e., dealing with anger, sexuality, and a feeling of weakness or vulnerability)—hence the dragon symbol. The main problem in dealing with these things stemmed from my tendency to totally identify with these feelings. When I was feeling angry, lustful, or weak I tended to actually *become* the feeling—losing to a large extent a deeper sense of the self that, yes, *experiences* feelings but *is not* the feeling. This total identification with an emotion tends to paralyze one before it. Gradually, however, I began to see (partly through this dream) that there was truly a deeper self that I could experience as a stabilizing factor in the situation.

Emotions and drives were present in me, but were *not me*. These things are even (in one sense) illusory in that they are temporary, they come and go. At the most brief experience of the True Self, the "I" or spiritual identity, I began to see that even some of the strongest emotions can disappear in "a puff of smoke." Of course, they will reappear and disappear many times, but the Self always remains.

A fascinating helper has certainly come to aid the young monk engaged in the tasks of his journey. There seem to be several levels of significance to the fact that his helper is a monkey. For one thing, dreams pun, and the words *monk* and *monkey* are very close to each

## A Monk's Dreams

other. The monkey may thus represent a sort of trickster side of him. He ends up laughing, and it is almost casual at the end—almost a joke. There is the feeling that the laughter of the monkey prince is part of what creates the perspective that makes the dragons go away.

The Japanese kimono relates the monkey prince to the Oriental tradition, perhaps because of the long Oriental tradition of monastic life. The monkey prince may also be related to the Hindu monkey hero-god Hanuman. In the ancient Sanskrit epic *Ramayana* many of Hanuman's exploits are told. As another monk, Thomas Merton, commented, Hanuman is at once a monkey, a god, and a successful fighter. One of Merton's experiences on his last trip, as he recounts it in *The Asian Journal*, gives us an amplification of the dreamer's monkey prince: "When we went up on the mountain from Swarg Ashram [in the Himalayas] I heard a great commotion in the tall trees and looked up to see marvelous gray apes with black faces crashing and swinging through the branches. They were huge, almost as big as people. Six or seven beautiful, funny Hanumans. It would be wonderful, to live in a hermitage with apes in the trees around it."[1]

This catches the perspective of lightness which the monkey prince in the dream brings to the dreamer. This is the kind of experience of monkeys and apes which most of us in urbanized worlds only have when we go to the zoo, where some of the biggest crowds gather around the monkeys and apes. Those are the crowds with the peals of laughter as people and monkeys "ape" each other, to the delight of both.

The young monk's struggle is a serious one for his journey, but the monkey prince's perspective on the struggle, as he throws his crown at the dragons almost playfully, is like a game of Frisbee. The serious work is serious, but at the same time it is "all a great joke." Such trickster helpers are likely to occur in dreams when the dreamer tries to become too holy without remembering that all of us are also partly instinct and nature. Then, in such forgetting, the individual is likely to flip to the opposite side and, as the monk says, *become* the dragons.

Somewhat later, the monk had another dream, which may, in part, elaborate some of the same themes. He called this dream "The Visitor from Heaven." It is helpful to know in reading of the dream that in his community a "visitation" occurs every two years. The abbot of the mother house visits the daughter house, interviews all in the community, then gives a report. The purpose is to help keep up discipline and observance. This is an even longer dream:

> There was going to be a visitation at the monastery, and the Abbot announced in Chapter that the regular visitor could not come, so Brother S. (one of the younger monks) would be conducting the visitation. Brother S. addressed the community in Chapter after he had spoken to all the monks. He said that there was some kind of intrigue going on in the monastery and that he intended to get to the bottom of it. I wondered what he meant and all the monks looked puzzled.
> 
> The scene changed: I am walking up a cobblestone path to a little cottage to visit a wise old man who can tell me all about my dreams. I enter his cottage, and he gets down a large old book in which he begins looking up dream symbols and things about dreams. I feel great affection for him, and I feel that he is very wise. He looks up from his book and tells me, "Everyone thinks that Brother S. is the visitor, but actually I (the old man himself) am the true visitor from Heaven."
> 
> I was then suddenly back in the monastery talking to one of the monks about the old man, telling him that the old man was the real visitor. The monk had heard nothing about the old man and looked at me in disbelief. As we were talking a young man—about 30 or so—came up to me. I knew immediately that this young man was the "visitor from Heaven," but had just taken on another form. He took both my hands in his and had a very comforting, loving presence about him.
> 
> At this point parts of the dream are hazy to me, but they amount to the "visitor" appearing and reappearing in several different forms—three, to be exact. Sometimes he was the old man, sometimes the 30-year-old and sometimes a baby or small boy. When he was in the form of the small boy, there was always a large group of devotees with him who recognized him as a spiritual master.
> 
> I was standing in a broad hall. It was something like a train station. There were many people standing around as if they were waiting, and they had loads of luggage with them. They were all from India and had on Indian garb, "saris" of many bright colors, etc. The "visitor" in the young boy form came down the hall with his throng of disciples. One devotee was carrying him. When they went by me, the young visitor looked at me and smiled with great affection and tenderness. He was a little Indian boy and had very big beautiful black eyes. I felt

that he understood and loved me perfectly and felt that he was my true spiritual master. The procession stopped at an Indian family that was standing beside me. They had three or four children and one (a little boy) was writhing on the floor and foaming at the mouth as if possessed by a demon.

The little master asked to be put down out of the arms of the devotee who was carrying him. The master said some kind of incantation in a strange language that I thought was Tibetan for some reason. The possessed boy stopped his movements immediately and sat up in his right mind. After a few moments, however, he threw himself down on the ground and started his movements again. The master leaned over to the parents, and they stooped down to hear him. He whispered, as if he didn't want the boy to hear, "He has wrath, but now that we understand his problem, he will gradually improve. Do not worry."

I was then in a large hall that I knew belonged to the little master. Many disciples of the master were walking down the hall, and I knew that we were going to visit the altars where the master worshipped. We arrived at the altars. In order to see them we had to walk down steep stairs that ran down the left side of the hall to a lower level. We went down many levels of stairs until we reached the altars. We reverently filed past the altars, but could not touch them because a golden rope separated us from them. There were many altars, and they had on them Buddhas, Hindu deities, Christian icons, crosses, Stars of David, etc.—about any type of religious image I could imagine.

There was one statue of a little man with fairy-like wings and a long droopy hat on. The figure was kneeling and facing the altars as if in worship. I knew that this statue represented the little master. I knew also that the master was on his way to the altars to destroy all the images. I heard a voice say, "You must get beyond your ideas of holy and unholy, of pure and impure." Even though I love all these images dearly, they must be destroyed—I thought.

I was then with a large group of disciples in another hall that belonged to the master. In the center of the hall was a large round "gazebo" (like a band would play on in a park). All the disciples started kneeling, facing the center of the gazebo. There was a space left in the center, and I knew that the master was going to appear there as the boy. In front of me was kneeling Brother X, whom I don't get along with at all. When I saw Brother X, I thought, "What a shame it is that we both have the same master, but we don't get along together." I began to feel so bad about this as I thought about it that I began to cry. I said, "Master, where are you now?" Suddenly he was there in front of me, but he was in the form of the 30-year-old man and nobody but I recognized him in that form.

He held my hands in his and said, "Remember when we first met on the highway?" I said, "Yes." He said, "Is it enough for you?" I said, "It's enough." He squeezed my hands very tightly. I woke up right away, and it was 1:30 a.m.

This dream is complicated, and we will only consider some of its possible meanings. The dream seems to concern the true meaning of "visitations" for the dreamer's spiritual life—the true visitation which matters is his personal relation with God and, as appears at the end of the dream, the effect of this relation on his relation to his community. It uses the symbol of the corporate visitations of his order to talk about the personal examinations he makes in order to help keep his soul's health in good order and observance.

The first odd thing about this symbolic visit is that, contrary to any actual possibility in the outer world, a very young brother appears to be the visitor. This may indicate that the dreamer, a young monk himself, is the visitor—or *appears to be* the visitor—who examines his own soul. Or it may simply use Brother S. to create some sense of puzzlement about how and what this visit is to be like.

At any rate, the dream soon shows that Brother S. is not really the visitor, but rather someone else, who appears first as a wise old man who knows about dreams—surely an affirmation that dream work is an appropriate part of wisdom and that this wisdom is available to the dreamer from within. The old man also associates himself with heaven: "I am the true visitor from Heaven." This is something like Jesus' statements about being the true bread from heaven. The old man of dreams consults an old book and lives on a cobblestone street, another association with an old way of living. This wise old helper is what Jung would call a Self image—that center and circumference of the psyche, who is the dream-maker and the one who calls people to wholeness. In Christian terminology this is an image of God at the center of the dreamer's being—even appearing in three forms in the dream, perhaps reminiscent of the Trinity.

The dreamer is then back in the monastery, trying to tell another monk who the real visitor is, but he is met with disbelief. The second form of the visitor appears even as they talk, this time as a thirty-year-old man. This may associate the visitor with the dreamer's own age, or, even more, with the age Jesus was when he began his ministry—perhaps as encouragement to trust this visitor, even if he's not *old* and wise. Developmentally, this age is frequently a major spiritual turning point. During the time when the visitor appears nearest the dreamer's age, he seems to be of the most direct comfort to the dreamer, actually touching him and holding his hands in a loving way.

Then the visitor regresses further in age in several scenes in which he reminds one of the young gurus from various Eastern religious traditions. The young guru casts a demon out of a little boy who is writhing and foaming on the floor. This scene evokes such healing narratives in Christian tradition as that of Matthew 17, after Jesus comes down from the Mount of Transfiguration. This little boy is healed, as in Scripture, but then he is thrown down again.

Here there may be an association with the dragon dream, where the monk spoke of one of the demon-dragons as his anger. Apparently by way of explanation about the return of the affliction, the little master says the afflicted boy "has wrath."

In his explanation of the dragon dream, the monk wrote that his dragons would of course "reappear and disappear many times," and this visitation dream probably comes after some more struggles with his anger. This dream, too, brings a humorous sense of perspective to the monk's anger, describing him as "writhing on the floor and foaming at the mouth." The young monk was unlikely to have expressed his anger in any such outward fashion, but the dream seems to point to his feeling like this on the inside. The reassurance of the monk's dream again is not to worry; the situation will gradually improve now that "we understand his problem." There is even a clue that the anger has already improved, as it is no longer represented by the huge dragon, but by a little boy. It is still a problem, but in a more differentiated mode.

The most fascinating scene in the dream is the one with all the religious images, which, though dearly loved, must be destroyed. Many spiritual writers from different traditions have commented that when one goes deeply enough into one's *own* religious tradition, one meets there others who have gone as deeply into *their* traditions. Ira Progoff, the "Jewish guru," as one friend called him, suggests the image of each of us going deeply into our own spiritual "well," and when we are deep enough, we encounter an underground stream common to all. None of this is to suggest that devotees leave their own tradition; the depth of one's own devotion accompanies the honor given to others.

Some such idea is suggested in the altars, which are reached by going "down steep steps" for "many levels of stairs." It suggests that a main thrust of the young monk's growth is to keep seeing that the images that are created, no matter how dear they are, are idols and not God. The scene seems both a powerful statement about the honor due all religious images (not just Christian ones) and at the same time an even stronger statement that all of them are to be transcended. Or, as Jesus said when confronted with a similar question about appropriate worship, "But the hour is coming, and now is when the true worshipers will worship the Father in spirit and truth, for such the Father seeks to worship him."[2]

Perhaps this scene, too, can be illuminated by a reference to Merton's *Asian Journal*. The day after Merton's first audience with the Dalai Lama, he reported a dream:

> Last night I dreamed that I was, temporarily, back at Gethsemani. I was dressed in a Buddhist monk's habit, but with more black and red and gold, a "Zen habit," in color more Tibetan than Zen. I was going to tell Brother Donald Kane, the cook in the diet kitchen, that I would be there for supper. I met some women in the corridor, visitors and students of Asian religion, to whom I was explaining I was a kind of Zen monk and Gelugpa together, when I woke up. It was 6 A.M. Time to get up.[3]

Merton then jots down "other recent dreams, dimly remembered," including this note: "How to get to the 'next place'?" A Gelugpa is one of the Tibetan Buddhist sects, the one to which the Dalai Lama belongs. Merton was in the Far East to speak to an interfaith conference and to study Hinduism and Buddhism. He had obviously been deeply moved by these encounters and spoke of the commonality of "monks" of various traditions and their relation to Marxism in the address he gave the day he died. For example, four days after the dream, in a letter he wrote to be circulated, he said in part:

> I am entirely occupied with these monastic encounters and with the study and prayer that are required to make them fruitful. I hope you

will pray for me and for all those I will be meeting. I am sure the blessing of God will be upon these meetings, and I hope much mutual benefit will come from them. I also hope I can bring back to my monastery something of the Asian wisdom with which I am fortunate to be in contact—but it is something very hard to put into words.[4]

Some transcendent vision of oneness seems implicit in another dream Merton reported ten days later, while in retreat at an estate beside the huge mountain Kanchenjunga. Merton's report and his interpretation are both in *The Asian Journal*:

Last night I had a curious dream about Kanchenjunga. I was looking at the mountain and it was pure white, absolutely pure, especially the peaks that lie to the west. And I saw the pure beauty of their shape and outline, all in white. And I heard a voice saying—or got the clear idea of: "There is another side to the mountain." I realized that it was turned around and everything was lined up differently; I was seeing it from the Tibetan side. This morning my quarrel with the mountain is ended. Not that it is a big love affair . . . but why get mad at a mountain? It is beautiful, chastely white in the morning sun—and right in view of the bungalow window.

There is another side of Kanchenjunga and of every mountain—the side that has never been photographed and turned into post cards. That is the only side worth seeing.[5]

Merton seems to be struggling toward the same kind of transcendent honor of all faiths to be attained by going around to the "other side" and seeing things from another standpoint, and he evidently wanted to bring home some of this "Asian wisdom" to his own monastery. As he stated this position in his last address, "So you respect the plurality of things, but you do not make them ends in themselves."[6]

Even with these amplifications from Merton's writing to explicate the meaning of the young monk's dream images, what could such a transcendent dream be saying to him specifically about his own life at the time he dreamed it? The clue seems to come in the next episode of the dream. Thereafter, in "another hall that belonged to the master," all this powerful God imagery gets brought right down to the daily life and stress of the brother the dreamer does not "get along with at all." The message stressed in this scene is that it is a "shame . . . that we both have the same master, but we don't get along together." The dreamer is so moved he cries and calls for the master. To carry out the dream's elaborate religious insights, the dreamer is called to face his own failure in a community relationship. This simple scene could almost be a simple paradigm of the needs of the whole world for peace and respect for others.

For this dreamer, as for all dreamers, this specific dream comes to heal him. The monk, by paying attention to his need for healing, is in line with the vision of "monastic therapy" Merton identifies as a basic idea in monasticism: "that you come to the monastery, first, to be cured. The period of monastic formation is a period of cure, of convalescence."[7]

The powerful healing ending of the dream, which awoke the dreamer in the middle of the night, is a true epiphany of the master. It is like the end of Job, where the Lord answered Job's complaint out of the whirlwind, simply by showing Job all the wonder and majesty of creation. After seeing and hearing God, the text suggests, Job can only despise himself and repent for questioning God.[8]

It is also like the two disciples who encountered the resurrected Jesus on the road to Emmaus; they said their "hearts burned within us while he talked to us on the road."[9] When the dreamer has encountered the master and remembered the past encounters, "it is enough."

# ▶15
# A Nun's Dreams

A series of powerful dreams came to a nun in her mid-thirties, whom we will call Terry, during the most difficult period of her life, as she struggled with a decision on whether to stay in her Franciscan religious order or leave it. She had been in religious life for sixteen years and still felt deeply committed to her vocation and to the vision of Saint Francis; but she felt that her community, most of whose members were much older and more conservative than she, was not living the vision which had first called her to her vows. What happens to the religious vow of obedience when obedience to the order seems to deny or vitiate one's relation to God?

During the period of this struggle and the dreams below, Terry continued to work in a parish, giving spiritual direction, pastoral counseling, and retreats. Yet her inner struggle expressed itself inwardly in depression, sometimes almost to despair. She had tried antidepressant medication, which helped some; but she really wanted to be healed and whole again, so she also continued to work with receiving counseling and spiritual direction, with her own prayer life, and with dreams and active imagination.

A dream that inspired her to seek outside help to get to a deep level with her dreams was this one, which resonates with a tale from ancient mythology:

> I was in a dreamlike state in which I saw a woman in a white, flowing dress, loose and beautifully white. But her face was black! She had some stuff on it. Her hands were white. She was screaming out in

long, painful screams—something about being captive and wanting release. Her cries were piercing and intense.

She called me over and asked me to go to a river and bring some special water. She handed me a bucket and gave me directions. I was also to bring a white cloth. This I brought first (before I went to the river). Then I started out for the water. It was much farther than I expected—a long trail through the woods.

Finally I came to the stream, but something prevented me from getting to it—a witch! She was in black and would not let me near the stream. I ducked into the woods and put on an outfit of light which sort of blinded her temporarily and allowed me to quickly get the water. I left it on until I was clear of her power (her area) and then kept walking, careful not to spill the water.

It began to thunder and lightning and rain. I pulled out a cape and covered myself and my bucket and kept going. When I finally arrived back at the place where the woman was, she had changed.

Time was different for her than for me—she was very old. She had grey hair, her face was still black and weak and frail. I quickly gave her the water saying: You didn't tell me about the witch! (feeling a little angry with her). "Oh, her," she said with a smile—seemed not to mean much to her. As she washed the black off and rinsed the cloth in the bucket, I noticed that the water stayed clear, was not blackened by the contents on the cloth washed into it. She soon had a white face again—her youthfulness restored.

This dream bears a striking resemblance to part of the story of Amor and Psyche from Greek mythology, a story which has been repeatedly told and interpreted in the twentieth century, frequently by Jungians.[1] Psyche means "soul," and the story is seen as the story of the human soul in its journey toward the Self, toward Olympus, toward God. In the story Psyche is assigned four different "impossible" tasks or ordeals by the goddess Aphrodite. Each time, she achieves the task by help from outside.

In the first task Psyche is required to sort out an enormous pile of varied seeds into separate piles by evening. She achieves this task with the help of a horde of ants.

For her second task Psyche must acquire some golden fleece from huge rams, who would surely crush her if she went among them. Again Psyche receives help to accomplish the task through a reed's suggestion that she wait until the rams are asleep and then gather the wisps of golden fleece from the briars.

In the third task Psyche is to bring water from the River Styx (which an eagle brings her), and in the fourth she is to go into the underworld and bring back a cask of beauty ointment (at which task a tower advises her what to take with her and especially what to do—to refuse to be distracted from her task, even by pathetic requests for help).[2] There may be elements of both these last two tasks in Sister Terry's dream, since she must fetch a special water and that water restores youthfulness to the dream woman.

The dream is complicated, but some aspects seem clear: first, the terrible pain expressed in the intense screaming at being captive and wanting release. This is a clarion call to go on a heroic journey from the captive place.

Two shadow parts of Terry appear in the dream—one, the captive dressed in white, but with "black stuff" on her face; the other, the witch in black who will not let Terry go down to the water. Since we do not have Terry's associations with these figures, we can only speculate that some opposites need to be reconciled in her and that something in her persona relation to the world needs to be cleaned up. The path to doing so is to "put on an outfit of light"—perhaps shine light onto the whole situation by increased consciousness. She must put on the armor of light in order to avoid the witch's power.

Psyche's last two tasks have been interpreted as representing the need to assimilate power (Erich Neumann), the need for focus (Robert Johnson) and emotional distance (Jean Bolen), and the need to learn to say no (both Johnson and Bolen) or to suspend the claims of what is close at hand for the sake of a distant goal (Neumann). These may well be clues for Terry's treasure, which she needs to find on her journey.

The dream imagery suggests that she has been somewhat unconscious (or has not *faced* up to something)—has been "in a dreamlike state." It will not be a "quick fix" ("It was much longer than I expected"), and she will have to go through the woods and face storms. Yet it also shows the urgency of her task, both in the screaming of the woman at the beginning of the dream and the weakness and frailty at the end. If she can bring the cleansing waters, though, the water will not be overcome with the darkness and the woman's youthfulness will be restored—a good prognosis.

This dream and her own confusion prompted her to seek counseling help with the avowed purpose of sorting out "what God wanted her to do"; perhaps even her initial goal is related to Psyche's first task in the myth—sorting out the jumbled seeds—which Psyche was able to do with the help of the instincts in the form of the ants. Terry's initial dream in counseling was a long one with lots of scenes that included the theme of *waiting* and with another promising ending. The dream ended with this scene:

> Then the scene shifted again and was with this group exploring old ruins or something. This one section was under water and we dove into this wonderful clear water to see this magnificent structure. It was in miniature and was greatly detailed and truly a work of art. We admired it and swam all around it under the clear water. We had looked at the other ruins—old and aged with time, in ruin before seeing the one under water.

The waters of clarity are still in her dreams, and this time she has taken the plunge to explore them.

The dreams that followed contained many images of violence, war, mutilation, and death. In outer life Terry struggled, on the one hand, with her feelings of loyalty to her original vows and to the charism of Saint Francis, the founder of her order, and on the other, with her sense of the rigidity and limitation of her specific branch of the community. Finally, with the encouragement of her spiritual director and to give herself some space and time, she wrote a formal letter asking her order for a year of exclaustration, which is a year's leave from connection with the order, for the purpose, as she told the council in the letter, of trying to "further identify and rid myself of those things which keep me from truly being pure of heart in my serious seeking of God's will in my life."

During the period when she struggled with whether to write the letter, one interesting but ordinary image appeared in two dreams. Just before she reached the decision to write it, she dreamed that she was supposed to change a tire, but she began screaming, "I CAN'T!" Though the subject matter of the dream was so ordinary—changing a tire—Terry's pain in the dream was extreme. Two weeks later, after she had written the letter, she had another dream, a part of which concerned changing tires:

> I recall being at the beach at this huge lake. There was an old car there which needed a lot of work. I started by jacking up the front, first one side, then the other, to change two of the tires. Anyway, the jack

slipped. The ground was rocky and not real level. There was no direct experience of being hurt in the dream, but I was really angry about it and frustrated. I was telling someone about it and they were going to help me. The car was sort of on the shore. I think part of it was in a couple of inches of water.

In outer life, she had begun to look for a car, and these two dreams bring her deep spiritual struggle right down to the nitty-gritty of ordinary life. The tire-changing image points toward her tasks of working on new ways of getting around in life on her own.

While she waited and worked to understand where her life needed to go, she had a dream which bears some similarity to Psyche's second task:

There was a group of us using this method for getting the wool from sheep. Two people would stand at either end of an oval shaped rope or some kind of line that was kept taught [sic] around their waists. The sheep would be inside the oval shape and the two would run back and forth, brushing the line against the sheep. We were talking about the disadvantage of this method—i.e., the wool could be no longer than the length of the distance, then there would be a fold in the wool. We were examining the wool. It was white, clean and soft.

In a way, Terry's dream seems almost like a parody of Psyche's task, which was to acquire golden fleece from the dangerous rams of the sun. Perhaps the "disadvantage" of her method is related to "running back and forth," which is what she felt as if she did all the time—both outwardly and emotionally. Yet there is a similarity, too, in that Psyche was advised to get the golden fleece by a trick, rather than a direct encounter. In outer life, she was feeling so tense, irritated, and driven that she felt a little crazy at times.

She was feeling much more "taut" (tightly drawn) than "taught" (learning skill) by her life experiences, but her misspelling suggests the learning. During this time, though Terry had not dreamed of *golden* fleece, a suggestion of Psyche's "gold" was added to her life through a remembered dream fragment of swimming in a very large swimming pool—Olympic-sized. Her association with this image was with the advice of a professional supervisor: "to go for her gold."

She was granted her exclaustration by the order, and she also (with difficulty) was able to confront her supervision group with her need to leave the group, after which she had this dream:

We were in this place—sort of like a big palace or mansion but open and with courtyard, pools, and huge statues—one of a lion I recall. The whole group of us had built the place from the ground up. We were a friendly and peaceful people and were now quite established and wealthy, I think. The dream was long and involved. I don't recall much about the middle, but we were very happy in that place.

Then there was talk of a "melt down" and the whole place was going to be destroyed. The various people were taking various courses of action. Some were staying in one part of the place, others were moving around, others preparing to leave, etc. People kept walking past the area with the pool and lion statue. The danger grew and our time grew shorter. I decided very serenely to sit down in a chair and wait for the end. I sat there and began saying: "The Lord is my Shepherd, I shall not want . . ." All was peaceful . . . so serene, I think one other woman was with me and wanted to do the same thing—she watches me and was anxious. Then I'd say: "I/we, no longer I, but Christ lives in me."

A helpful theory to elaborate Terry's journey during this phase is that of the *temenos*, the ancient Greek word for the space surrounding a sacred area, temple, or church. Jung identified the temenos as a symbol of the Self, with the psychological function of providing a protective structure for the integration of personality. Neil Canavan has explicated the symbols connected with the temenos. He focuses on the threefold pattern which occurs when a change or reintegration of personality is required, when the old temenos no longer adequately contains the personality: the loss of the old, the suffering period after the loss, and the reconstitution of a new temenos.[3] Obviously, this threefold pattern resembles the hero monomyth, and the temenos imagery becomes an aid to identifying the stage of the journey.

Mandalas, caves, cities, sacred precincts, gardens, nests, prisons—all have been identified as temenos symbols. The loss of the old temenos can come in dreams of huge, threatening waves, storms, bombs, or the end of the world. The images of the middle stage are much like those in the middle stage of the hero journey, and the new temenos can again be represented by any containing imagery.

Jungian analyst Robert L. Moore points out that the counselor's consulting room can be a temporary temenos for the client engaged in the middle stage of the hero journey, thus providing a "therapeutic space" for the healing process to take place. He compares Eliade's work on *sacred space,* Jung's alchemical idea of the *closed vessel,* and Victor Turner's understanding of the *transition phase* in which transformation takes place. He then compares those ideas to the experience of psychotherapy and the necessity for there to be ritual space in which transformation can take place. He writes: "I anticipate that we will soon come to a fresh appreciation of the role of the ritual leader as the steward of the thresholds and boundaries of transformatived space in all human cultures—past, present, and future."[4]

Terry's imprisonment in the first dream described in this chapter feels like an old temenos that no longer contains her in a creative way. The suggestion of finding a new temenos lies in the second dream. As Terry explored old, aged ruins, she found a "magnificent structure" underwater. Perhaps this suggested that the new temenos was there, but as yet unconscious for Terry—buried in the water.

Understanding this dream in terms of temenos imagery, we can say that she was at first in the castle, a strong Self-temenos image, but that the basic center of energy in that old temenos was being destroyed—melted down. Though she has as yet no new temenos to contain her, while she awaits the destruction of the old, the Lord as shepherd and the Christ within are strong helpers. With her focus on them through the dream prayer, she can even comfort the anxious shadow part of herself who "wanted to do the same" serene praying and waiting.

Her own associations with the dream imagery of the meltdown began with the characterization of herself as a "no-nuke person," who feared the dangers of nuclear energy. Yet the most prominent energy she felt toward the dream was toward the incredible serenity at the end.

A noteworthy image because of later developments is the statue of the lion—the only statue Terry identifies in the dream castle.

In the year that followed she faced, first, taking care of all sorts of outer details she had never worked with before. She had to find a place to live, a car, and she had to deal with all sorts of issues she had never before dealt with. As she struggled with these tasks, she felt tired, confused, and resistant to the future. Just as she would feel the most exhausted, her dreams would produce strong, helpful shadow figures, such as a dream of an old high school classmate, whom she described as athletic, adventuresome, and open to whatever nature holds. She also dreamed of Joan of Arc, and of going on trips, marches, and running races. The psyche produced strong compensatory imagery for her road of trials.

As she neared the end of her first year of exclaustration, she was scheduled to play the guitar for the Sunday mass on the Feast of Saint Clare, companion of Saint Francis, a saint whose life had been nearly as important to her as Francis's had. When she heard the song she had sung at her own final vows, "Come Back to Me with All Your Heart," she wept painfully, feeling that she belonged nowhere anymore. Being a sister was her true vocation; as she put it, "An ex-nun is *not* me!" Yet, unable to reach any firm decision, she asked for and received a second year of exclaustration.

She had a number of dreams of death in the weeks that followed; something in her was dying, but she could not be sure what it was. At a Transitus service (a service celebrating Saint Francis's death), she played the part of the mime representing Francis dying and was deeply moved by the experience. After that she dreamed a kind of rebirth dream:

> We're in this place and I'm trying to call Motor Vehicle Division to find out about my license which expires that day. I can't get thru. It is a place like [her old mother house] or somewhere where there's lots of people. I keep trying to get thru and either have the wrong number or can't get them for some reason.
>
> Then we're sitting around on the ground and this guy is explaining about this engine or something mechanical. He's very proud of it, just brought it over (from? . . .). I'm not really interested but ask if it's Turbo and he says yes. He's passing parts of it around for us to see. Then we're going thru this narrow passage. It's crawling thru the earth and is very narrow. We all crawl thru and sit down in this more open area—still underground.
>
> I get tired of listening and bored and decide I really have to go and use the phone to find out about my license. So I go back thru the narrow opening. It's very very small and difficult to crawl thru. I'm concerned about suffocating and imagine what my body would look like after having died in there—blue and swollen and all. I try to dig little areas in the earth and rock to grasp into with my fingers and for them who will be following me as they come thru. I get out finally and after much struggle and go to a phone (booth?) on the top of this hill.

Another dream the next night suggested that, though she was going on with the journey, she was not "charting." She had formerly been a nurse who charted the status and treatment of patients, and this image of not charting seemed to her to represent her not paying enough attention to what was going on. This probably connects to her fear in the dream of losing her driver's license, the license which enables her to get around independently in life. The dream ends without her completing the call to the license division. Somehow, though all the possibilities are there, the dream suggests that she is not taking charge.

Perhaps it is an encouragement to dig out from underground, even though it is difficult and she fears suffocating. She needs to dig out the earth and rock with her bare fingers to make it. Some of her attempts to sort out her own vocation felt like this image. She was thus, during this period, still engaged in a task like Psyche's first ordeal—sorting out a seemingly impossible number of problems, all of which she felt deep conflict about. She was aware that the order seemed a way toward death for her, though going back felt much safer. She knew that her sisters would be hurt more if she left, but she felt increasingly that leaving was all she could do.

She worked very hard in the next weeks to sort out her own path, her relationships, her work situation, and what she felt called to for the future. As if to confirm that she was not alone in her work, a month later she dreamed of lions again, this time alive:

> I'm coming down from a high mountain along this path. Sides of mountain are rocky. As I get about half way down a lioness comes bounding toward me. She is huge—large paws—5–6" in diameter. She's playful I realize and say to myself, "Oh, yeah! lions don't attack people." She continues to go along with me on my left side as I continue walking. Then the lion comes along—bounding playfully, like his mate. They both follow me along the path as I proceed down the mountain.

The lions have come to life, whereas earlier she had only dreamed of a statue of a lion. Perhaps her instinct had been frozen—or even under a spell, like the animals in *The Lion, the Witch, and the Wardrobe* before they were brought to life again.[5] It is fitting that she, who was so devoted to the patterns of Saint Francis, should be accompanied by these powerful animal helpers.

For some reason, perhaps in part because of the strength, both feminine and masculine, represented by these strong instinctual helpers, in the following months Terry began to face things and see more clearly. She saw how much she wanted to belong to a community and yet how impossible it was for her to return to her own order. Though she still was uncertain precisely how her religious vocation was to be exercised, she had enough clarity at the end of her next year to leave her order formally. She had investigated other orders to which she might transfer, but was unsure whether she should join them.

Yet she felt strong enough to be able to wait until she was certain of her direction. Meanwhile, she continued her deep contemplative prayer, watching her dreams, making retreats, and generally following the regular practices so dear to her. She continued her outer work of counseling and giving spiritual direction. She still found it difficult to wait, but she was sure that waiting on God was the way to clarity for her.

# 16

# Prayer and Active Imagination

The last series of dreams are those of an Australian religious sister. Some of the dreams appeared in *Symbols of Transformation in Dreams,* and the others carry her story forward. The last of these dreams is particularly helpful because of the many ways she worked with it to unravel its meaning for her, even to encountering a strange character, a shark within.

In some of our earlier discussion of her dreams, we focused on her encounter with a conservative animus part of her inner masculine. The first one showed fear and conflict:

> I go to visit a sick and very conservative bishop. I even take Holy Communion to him, but he says, "No." I take the Blessed Sacrament home.

As we noted, this sister was authorized by her church to administer the sacrament of communion, but it would have been unusual for a woman—who cannot at present be ordained under the rules of her church—to take communion to a bishop. At the time of the dream, however, this sister was being requested to help other women and men in ways which to her own conservative leanings were still considered the sole prerogative of ordained priests. She had spent a year in special study and renewal to equip her to give such help, but the dream seems to picture her inner conflict between two parts of herself—her conscious ego and a "sick and very conservative" authoritative animus figure.

A year later another dream pointed to some reconciliation between these two parts:

> I dreamed I was preparing for ordination. We were a mixed group of men and women, and it was up to us to decide if we would go ahead. At the last minute I was confused. We were in the church waiting to begin the service for ordination, and I went over and asked to see the Monsignor. I needed to confirm my decision with someone, and he was the teacher of the class. We talked, and I told him of my doubts. He didn't say much. Finally I said, "Do you feel I'm right in going ahead?" He said, "Yes." I was relieved, and we returned to the ceremony, being late. We got there just at the end of the queue for imposition of hands. Monsignor laid hands on my head.

This dream again shows her doubts, this time in the dream ego, but here the animus figure, a conservative monsignor she knew in her outer life, blesses her decision to "go ahead," this time expressed in the ritual of ordination. In her outer life as a result of this dream, the sister felt some of the peaceful resolution and relief the dream suggests.

More challenges were coming her way, however, and another dream came to her to push her further than the previous two. She remained lacking in confidence in many situations in her life, even though she was sure that it was this very fear that made her less effective when she did venture into a situation which seemed threatening to her. She had been doing spiritual direction with some lay people and with a few religious sisters, but then one day she received a message that a local Jesuit would like to see her for spiritual direction, counseling, and dream work. Her feelings of inadequacy surfaced again. The fact that he was a *Jesuit* made it difficult for her to consider the possibility of *her* being *his* spiritual director. Would she say yes or no to him? That night she dreamed:

> I climbed into my car. It was as if I was about to drive away from the Clifts' seminar to return to my home one hundred miles away. A couple I knew had hoped to attend the seminar, but got sick and had to miss. I got settled in the car, fixing the gear, etc., when I looked up. There was a neatly dressed young man (collar and tie) standing beside the passenger door in the front of the car. It seemed the couple had asked earlier if he could get a ride with me, but they weren't there to

introduce him. He startled me, and I felt a little fearful to let him into the car to travel with me, but it seemed I would have to do that. I wasn't certain he was their friend; he may have been a stranger!

Reflecting on the dream, she felt it referred to the Jesuit's request, which was certainly what had grabbed her psychic attention from the day before. The couple she knew in the dream were people she had given spiritual direction and counseling to. In the last sentence of the dream, the question of discernment is raised: is the neatly dressed young man a helper or a tempter? After pondering this question, it seemed to her that he was a positive animus figure. He wanted to "take a front seat" in her life, but she was fearful of letting him in. It was this same fear that often held her back, almost crippling her at times. Although she did not report this fact, it is our guess that a significant help to her decision was the image that she was just leaving "the Clifts' seminar" as the dream began. She had in fact just attended a seminar we gave, and it is our guess that she realized afresh how much she already knew about inner spiritual work with dreams.

At any rate, as she mulled over the dream her fear seemed to recede somewhat. She phoned the Jesuit, told him something of her hesitation, but expressed her willingness to share his journey. Their first session together went well. She said most of her fear was gone, and she was able to focus truly on him.

That dream and what followed from it gave her light for many occasions in her life when feelings of inadequacy gripped her. She could recall her positive animus figure waiting to take a front seat in her car. From this time on she became increasingly able to claim her own authority by sharing with others who wanted her help the treasure of what she had learned. She had brought a professional treasure home and was sharing it with the community of her world.

As with all of us, though, there were other aspects of her journey going on at the same time. Another part of her task was presented to her by dreams which concerned her feminine nature. She realized she needed to reexamine her attitudes toward sexuality. She had grown up with negative attitudes and guilt which had stunted her growth toward sexual maturity. She needed more inner freedom to relate to her own femininity and to other people. She took a workshop on sexuality, during which she dreamed:

> I guide into a church a young woman who is blind. I try to find a seat for her, but all the seats are wobbly and old—so too is the floor of this dilapidated church building. I find a chair for her, but there is a step just behind it, and I fear she may move slightly and fall, but there doesn't seem to be any safer place in the church. She's very dependent on my putting her in the best, safest, most satisfactory place in the church.

This dream showed her just what her relation to her shadow was—a blind woman staying with a dilapidated set of attitudes. This dream gave her the courage to find "the best, safest, most satisfactory place in the church" and claim it for her own. She did not want to leave her chosen celibate way of life, but neither did she want to stay blind and sit in a wobbly old place.

Two years later, this time during a seminar on sexual morality, she dreamed:

> A child and I were sitting looking out a window of something like a guest house when I saw a koala in a tree outside. I felt really excited. I drew the boy's attention to it. It looked like a big gray tabby cat without a tail. It then seemed to walk out on a limb, which I could not see. It looked like he was walking up into fresh air, but I presumed it must have a fine limb that we couldn't see.

After she had this dream, the sister wrote in her journal, using the method of dialoguing with the koala. The little animal, which was warm, soft, and cuddly, yet had claws, symbolized for her the affective area of her life. The koala, which sleeps away the day, represented to her her own femininity, which had been, so to speak, put to sleep for many years.

As the two dialogued about the invisible tree limb, she realized that the seminar had caused to surface within her a fear that she might be going "out on a limb" with her newfound sense of freedom. Even realizing her fear, she decided she simply did not want to return to her old attitudes. Instead, she wanted to continue to develop to full potential the warmth and love that was deep within her. The transience of a guest house would seem to indicate that this fear of "being out on a limb" was not a permanent thing.

Six months later she dreamed:

I was in a big college and while everyone was quietly engaged in work, the superior was outside having fun. He was waltzing around with a koala in his arms. In fact, he tried to get a big matronly lady to dance with him, but she was bashful, so he then took the koala in his arms.

The sister understood from the dream that the "superior" in her needed to play and dance. There needed to be a closer relationship between her masculine leadership qualities and her own feminine warmth. The dream pointed her this way, but she still was not ready to dance; the big matronly lady holds back. Only the koala dances with the superior.

A number of the themes from her life subsequently came together in this dream:

I was in a dinghy and a shark got in the boat. I feared being attacked. The shark heard a tape recording of a woman's voice and was giving attention to that. I jumped out of the boat and a man grabbed me. I was safely out but the man fell in the water and the shark attacked him. He was very brave and sat astride the shark and began cutting round its neck with tin clippers. I wondered if he'd die in the effort. He seemed to be succeeding in severing the head. I woke in horror.

After writing the dream down, she tried what she called "dream reentry," that is, she tried in a waking meditation time to go back into the dream. She says that she went back into the dream, "becoming" the shark. Its power was significant to her—being the biggest fish, the "kingpin." Then she became the macho guy—big, brave, strong, skillful, top dog—overpowering the shark. Then she became herself in the dream—a feminine figure, terrified of the shark, wanting nothing to do with it.

Ten weeks later she went to a dream dance workshop, where with music and creative movement she again became each of the symbols in the shark dream. She said a profound change happened in her. In becoming the shark she realized that the shark was not attacking, but simply wanted to be friends. She was overwhelmed with sadness at the aggressive attack on the shark, but in being the shark she also realized it need not be dead. It was deeply wounded, but time would heal it. The shark was a part of her no longer to be feared; rather she had fallen in love with her shark. It was as if, having refused earlier to dance with the superior and the koala, the undifferentiated power within her showed up as a shark. In her terror, she tended to call up her masculine power principle to try to kill the shark; but she was finally learning to dance with her power.

A few days later she discussed the shark with a counselor, and together they reflected on when she made the decision to cut off her body (the wounding of the shark). She wrote of this work:

> I realized that in childhood I'd enjoyed some sexual pleasure with other kids, believed that seriously sinful, couldn't bring myself to tell that in Confession, carried that burden for two or three years, living in constant fear of dying and dropping into hell. At about the age of nine, I finally told the priest in Confession. He was kind, but when I came out of the Confessional, I made a very definite decision: from that moment on, I would *never* allow myself to enjoy my body. Even my fantasy life would be utterly controlled. At that moment of decision I had cut my own throat, cutting off my body and spending my life living out of my head. That was the wounding.

This was the guilt she had carried for so long—the guilt of having a body! The shark was a powerful enough symbol (and she had developed enough courage to face its power) that she could feel both the power and the sadness of trying to destroy it. For months leading up to that time, she had been very aware of her body and feelings being bound up, and she had been using the biblical image of Lazarus in the tomb in prayer, saying the mantra "Unbind her and let her go free." In working with the shark dream, she felt this unbinding gradually happening. She began to use music and movement in her prayers, and she would dance the death and resurrection of Lazarus.

During this period she had given a workshop and gotten a lot of affirmation, which was pretty heady stuff. She had come a long way from her fears of claiming her own ability to help others, but she in turn might be nearing some inflation or hubris—the other extreme. She was enjoying the feeling of being a "big fish" and being praised by others—maybe enjoying it a bit too much?

So she took her shark to prayer, simply sitting in Jesus' presence with the shark on her lap. Very soon in her active imagination the shark was creatively moving through the water; she was the shark and was touched by the beauty there and by her capacity to go deep. She realized that her inward journey had opened up a depth for her, along with a capacity to accompany others on their journey in the depths. Then Jesus was moving through the water, and he and the shark were playing affectionately. Then, she says, "I was Jesus dancing Jesus' resurrection. Then I was the shark dancing the shark's resurrection. This was a transforming moment for me—an experience of the transcendent. I was in touch with power, beauty, and depth—such beautiful gifts from the Lord." After this, she drew the shark and put it up on her wall.

Each of these modes of active imagination with the dream symbol of the shark not only led her to increased understanding, but also put her directly in touch with the power she had feared so long. It is of interest that the symbol of the shark is an important one in the Pacific, where she lives, and some general amplification of that symbol from Pacific lore enriches her shark image even more.

In the Hawaiian culture hundreds of objects and natural forces are imbued with symbolic meaning, and the shark, or *mano,* is well at the top of the list even in present-day Hawaii. For some Hawaiians, the shark is an *aumakua,* or ancestor god, in animal form; for others, it is just an object, but one to which many associations cling. In that tradition, sharks can be either evil or good: "The two-pronged association exists today. To Hawaiians the shark may be, symbolically: bravery, daring, strength, a chief; benevolence, protection, rescue. Or: fright, danger, destruction, death."[1]

Part of the positive association with the shark comes from the tradition that when the first Hawaiians sailed to Hawaii from Tahiti, "They were guided over the desolate wastes like beloved children by a single great guide, the shark named Kalahiki."[2] It was probably this tradition which James Michener reaches back to in *Hawaii,* in which Teura, the wise old woman guide for the sailors, speaks repeatedly with Mano, her "personal god."[3] We find it fascinating that Hawaiian dream lore and tradition come so close to the interpretations of the dream shark made by the Australian sister.

By relating to her dream shark, she had truly freed that which had been bound in her since she was nine years old, when she had, as she puts it, "cut her own throat." She even celebrated her dance in her

Silver Jubilee mass a month later! The image of her dancing that freedom at her Silver Jubilee mass is a moving example of one more hero task completed and shared with her sisters. Each of her journeys made her more truly human and thus more truly able to help others on their journeys to their true humanity.

# Afterword

It must be obvious that we think people are continually being lured forward on hero journeys, which are also journeys toward increased consciousness and responsibility. We see the path of individuation as the path of human and spiritual growth, a task to which all are called and which continues throughout life with many phases and turnings. The end of the road is never in sight when a given journey begins, and the way is fraught with terrors and dangers. We might say that the task is not for the faint of heart, except that it seems all of us are faint of heart as we begin new journeys. The task is for those who choose to go.

As Jung puts it: "In myths the hero is the one who conquers the dragon, not the one who is devoured by it. And yet both have to deal with the same dragon. Also, he is no hero who never met the dragon, or who, if he once saw it, declared afterwards that he saw nothing."[1] Of course, as Jung adds, the completed journey gives the hero faith and trust in the ability to tackle future threats, an inner certainty of being capable of self-reliance, of being a unified person.

Laurens van der Post, in one of his novels, portrays a young woman who was helped to achieve this kind of personal unity by an aunt and uncle who simply loved her into her integrity: "Almost without her knowing, the love of her aunt and uncle had turned her into a disciplined and emancipated version of her militant and rebellious childhood self. That was the wonder of it to her. Nothing had been imposed on her, yet she had developed a keep sense of direction, obedience, and dedication to the freedom and responsibility of being herself."[2] Yet, as this novel shows, and as life itself demonstrates to all, even with helpers the choice is still with the hero—as an old saying puts it, the choice to become who one *is*.

Choice itself is the great biblical task: choose this day whom you will serve. Dante portrayed in his *Divine Comedy* the effects of the choices we make. As one writer puts it, in Dante "no one is sent to Hell. Hell is what each person chooses."[3] Judgment itself is the choice of each individual soul. It has been suggested that the painting of the Last Judgment by Michelangelo in the Sistine Chapel is not a portrayal of Christ as a terrible judge, but a terrible drama of human choice. C. S. Lewis has portrayed the same kind of choice in *The Great Divorce*, where people in hell can catch a bus to heaven any time they choose, and they can stay there. The scenes in the book portray why most people do not choose to stay.[4] The same motif of choice is found in the parable of the separation of the sheep from the goats in the Gospel of Matthew.[5]

Whenever one's world becomes more complicated than one's world view can permit or understand, one is called to go on a hero journey. At its deepest, this is the hero journey of redoing one's theology. When the experience of life gets beyond one's understanding of God, one must find a new and larger theology or else say that God is dead, which is in itself a new theology. From our own theistic belief that God is always "larger" and more than anyone can know, it would be our position that the journey toward truth is always the journey toward God.

The monomyth pattern of the hero journey can help one make sense of the boredom before and the terror during each journey of growth. In journeys large and small there is help for the hero who finds the courage to put a hand to the plow, and much of that help can come through dreams. The monomyth can illumine the dreams, and the dreams can inspire the journey. Becoming the person one can become through these dreams and journeys is the meaning of the hero quest in all times and in each human life.

Even more, as we have suggested, there is meaning for the whole human community in each member's increments of heroic consciouness. The return of the hero with the treasure is a return which blesses not the hero alone, but the world. John Mattern, a Jungian analyst in Zurich, says that the true hero (or the truly heroic ego) is the one that survives the death of its power attitude. This is the ego which, in Jungian terms, is operating on behalf of the larger Self, not solely on behalf of its own power-for-itself. Mattern says that when this occurs successfully, there is new psychic energy available for the life process.[6]

We have tried to demonstrate the truth of this, even in very "small" heroisms. At first glance it may seem absurd to claim that one woman's financial responsibility, for example, is a task to help the world; but personal responsibility by each member is the greatest gift it is possible to give. We are all members of one another, and, as John Donne said so memorably, no one is an island; we are all parts of one another. More and more people in the world are realizing that all our actions affect one another as the consciousness of "one world" is increased. Even the small treasures of consciousness help the increase of consciousness so needed in our world.

# Appendix: Exercises for Reflection

Participants at hero journey seminars have found it helpful to remember, reflect, and journal about their own experiences with the various topics and stages discussed in this book. They may be used in a variety of ways, repeated many times to reflect on different life events, stories, or dreams, and written about for whatever length of time one chooses. They are designed, as are all the suggestions in the book, as ways of helping the journaler become more conscious.

## Story

Reflect on a remembered childhood story or fairy tale, a favorite one that either you read or was read or told to you—but one that stayed with you in some way—one that grabbed your imagination early in life. Write or outline the story. After you have outlined or written the story, look at it as if it were a dream. How would you interpret its symbolic significance in your life? Does it suggest some pattern of your typical behavior? Does it point to a deep longing of your heart or a goal of yours—perhaps even one you have almost forgotten? *Listen* to the story with open ears to learn its message for you.

Reflect on stories of communities of which you are a part—family, religion, club, region, tribe, race, nation, world. Write the stories that you have read or been told. Some of them may be beyond words, but nonetheless implicit in the community's mores. How have these stories affected you? Have you followed them—consciously or unconsciously? Have you rebelled against them? Are they still a part of who you understand yourself to be? Do you want them to be? What effect do these stories have on you and your life and values today? Seeing them objectively, do you still choose them?

### Call to Adventure

Reflect on a remembered experience of a longing or a call or vocation to do something new or risky or promising. Maybe the "promise" made little or no outward sense, but some "twinge" pulling at you from within intrigued you. Maybe you were thrust into a journey by outer circumstances not of your choosing. Whatever the method by which you were called, write it and then reflect on any current meaning it has in your life. If it has been lost from your life, would you like to reconsider any aspect of it? Is there any way in which a part of it might still be relevant for you, even if the original call is not?

### Crossing the Threshold

Reflect on a remembered separation—successful or not. The memory may be a mixture of joy and pain. Were you a reluctant hero? How did you try to build your courage? Did someone else help? Or did you make a kind of "inward boast"? If you did, was it a "foolish child's boast" or anchored in some genuine longing or hope—anchored in a possibility of reality you intended to carry out? Or did you remember a promise of value that you wanted to live? If you have been unable to cross a threshold over which you feel called, what hinders you? If you failed to cross a threshold over which you once felt called, can you now discern any meaning for your life in remembering the call? How might it live for you now? How might your failures in courage now be overcome?

### Helpers and Tempters

Reflect on a remembered helpful person or "friendly animal" type. What did they help save you from? What happened if you didn't listen? Are there helpers from stories or dreams who continue to influence you or the way you think or react to life? Do you remember a difficulty you had discerning whether someone was a help or a danger to your life's journey? What tempters did you listen to or follow? What effect has that had on your life? What prompted you to give in to the tempters? What can you learn from that about your future?

## Road of Trials

Reflect on a remembered dark period. Can you now discern anything helpful from it? Did you fall into despair of ever escaping from the darkness and claiming a place for yourself in life beyond the dark time? Did you travel through some dangers and not get caught by them? Did you escape from any symbolic prisons? Did you literally or figuratively learn something new about yourself? Did you become someone new? Did you become stronger in any way? If you failed a test, do you now see some helpful lesson to be learned from that?

Reflect on a remembered achievement. What treasure did you find? What imprisoned part of yourself did you recover or set free? What battles did you fight? What dragons did you slay? Were you tortured or mutilated? Did you have an experience which felt like dying? How did you integrate the "new you"? Did you experience a new and larger perspective? What happened in your world afterward as you tried to live it out? Did you face the danger of hubris, or identifying with your achievement instead of relating to it?

## Rites of Passage

Reflect on rituals you have experienced. Have community or religious rituals been meaningful for you? Explore the reasons they helped or failed you. Do you see meaning in their success or failure in your life? Have you been impoverished by the failure of ritual? Are there rituals that would be meaningful for you now? Are they available? If not, how might you ritualize important transitions in your own life? Have you experienced spontaneous rituals in your life or in your dreams or fantasies? What is their significance for you?

## Return

Reflect on a remembered return from a hero journey. Were you afraid or reluctant to make the return over the threshold? Did the world seem so different that you felt you could not return? Did anyone know you were a hero? Did you know it? Was it all right if no one else knew? How did you react differently to your world than you did before your consciousness was raised? Can you see that your new awareness or strength is useful to the world? What are the difficulties you experienced in rejoining your world? Did you come back to the old place and know it in new ways? What was the meaning of your journey for you and for others?

# Notes

### Introduction

1. Joseph Campbell, *The Hero with a Thousand Faces* (Princeton, N.J.: Princeton University Press, 1949; 2d ed., 1968).
2. Joseph L. Henderson, "Ancient Myths and Modern Man," in *Man and His Symbols*, ed. Carl G. Jung and (after his death) M.-L. von Franz (Garden City, N.Y.: Doubleday, 1964); Thayer A. Greene, *Modern Man in Search of Manhood* (New York: Association Press, 1967); Erich Neumann, *The Origins and History of Consciousness* (New York: Harper & Brothers, 1962); John A. Sanford, *The Man Who Wrestled with God* (King of Prussia, Pa.: Religious Pub. Co., 1974); Polly Young-Eisendrath, *Hags and Heroes* (Toronto: Inner City Books, 1984).
3. Jean Dalby Clift and Wallace B. Clift, *Symbols of Transformation in Dreams* (New York: Crossroad, 1985).

### Chapter 1: Living a Story

1. C. G. Jung, *Symbols of Transformation*, trans. R.F.C. Hull, vol. 5 of *The Collected Works of C. G. Jung* (Princeton, N.J.: Princeton University Press, 1956), p. xxiv.
2. Ibid., p. xxv.
3. Unpublished lecture, American Association of Pastoral Counselors Annual Meeting, New Orleans, May 1, 1987.
4. Ira Progoff, *At a Journal Workshop* (New York: Dialogue House Library, 1975) and *The Practice of Process Meditation* (New York: Dialogue House Library, 1980).
5. Unpublished lecture, American Association of Pastoral Counselors Regional Meeting, Denver, October 11, 1985.
6. Big Bill Neidjie et al., *Australia's Kakadu Man* (Darwin: Resource Managers, 1986), p. 64.

7. Laurens van der Post, *Yet Being Someone Other* (Harmondsworth, England: Penguin Books, 1982), p. 12.

### Chapter 2: The Monomyth

1. C. G. Jung, *The Development of Personality*, trans. R.F.C. Hull, vol. 17 of *The Collected Works of C. G. Jung* (New York: Pantheon Books, 1954), paragraphs 318 and 321.
2. Otto Rank, *The Myth of the Birth of the Hero and Other Writings* (New York: Vintage Books, 1946).
3. Flannery O'Connor, *The Habit of Being*, ed. and with an introduction by Sally Fitzgerald (New York: Random House, 1980), p. 126.
4. C. G. Jung, *Two Essays on Analytical Psychology*, trans. R.F.C. Hull, vol. 7 of *The Collected Works of C. G. Jung* (New York: Pantheon Books, 1966), paragraph 72.
5. James A. Hall, *Clinical Use of Dreams* (New York: Grune & Stratton, 1977), pp. 147–48.
6. It seems appropriate here to note that we do not agree with Campbell's conclusions about Christianity—particularly with what Martin E. Marty calls Campbell's "strange prejudice." Marty says of Campbell in the January 15, 1988, issue of his newsletter *Context*: "he could be fair to all religions but his own since-abandoned childhood Catholicism. It is interesting that many syncretists, synthesists, or searchers after gods and goddesses show amazing patience with all the deities except those close to home." In his 1987 essay in the *San Francisco Jung Institute Library Journal* (vol. 7, no. 4), "Joseph Campbell's Theory of Myth," Robert A. Segal writes: "Far closer to Nietszche than to Jung, Campbell, in polar contrast, castigates traditional Christianity generally *as* institutionalized and therefore psychologically impotent, damns his childhood Catholicism above all, revels in the demise of Christianity as a whole, and sees no need for a substitute for at least organized religion." We might add also that we do not follow all of C. G. Jung's efforts at doing theology. See Wallace B. Clift's *Jung and Christianity* (New York: Crossroad, 1982).
7. Erich Neumann, *The Origins and History of Consciousness* (New York: Harper & Brothers, 1962), p. 131.
8. Donald F. Sandner, "The Symbolic Life of Man," in *The Differing Uses of Symbolic and Clinical Approaches in Practice and Theory: Proceedings of the Ninth International Congress for Analytical Psychology, Jerusalem, 1983*, ed. Luigi Zoja and Robert Hinshaw (Zurich: Daimon Verlag, 1986), p. 347. The other two archetypal principles of symbolic healing Sandner identifies are the return to the origin and the management of evil.
9. Janice Hocker Rushing, "Mythic Evolution of 'The New Frontier' in Mass Mediated Rhetoric," *Critical Studies in Mass Communiction* 3, no. 3

(September 1986): 288. We are indebted to Lucy Clifthorne for calling our attention to this provocative and challenging article.

## Chapter 3: The Human Journey

1. Arnold van Gennep, *The Rites of Passage,* trans. Monika B. Vizedom and Gabrielle L. Caffee (Chicago: University of Chicago Press, 1960).
2. Mircea Eliade, *Rites and Symbols of Initiation* (New York: Harper & Row, 1965), pp. x, 131.
3. Louise Carus Mahdi, Steven Foster, and Meredith Little, eds., *Betwixt and Between: Patterns of Masculine and Feminine Initiation* (La Salle, Ill.: Open Court, 1987), p. xii.
4. Joseph L. Henderson, *Thresholds of Initiation* (Middletown, Conn.: Wesleyan University Press, 1967), p. 14.
5. Victor Turner and Edith Turner, *Image and Pilgrimage in Christian Culture: Anthropological Perspectives* (Oxford: Basil Blackwell, 1978), p. 15.
6. Joseph L. Henderson, "Ancient Myths and Modern Man," in *Man and His Symbols,* ed. Carl G. Jung and M.-L. von Franz (Garden City, N.Y.: Doubleday, 1964), p. 125. Compare the first of the twelve steps of Alcoholics Anonymous.
7. C. G. Jung, *The Archetypes and the Collective Unconscious,* trans. R.F.C. Hull, vol. 9(1) of *The Collected Works of C. G. Jung* (New York: Pantheon Books, 1959), paragraph 261.
8. Joseph Campbell, *The Hero with a Thousand Faces* (Princeton, N.J.: Princeton University Press, 1949), p. 256.
9. Leonel L. Mitchell, *The Meaning of Ritual* (New York: Paulist Press, 1977), p. 9.
10. Elinor J. Dickson, *Transformation of Consciousness: Therapy and Soul-Making* (Toronto: Regis College, 1987), pp. 13–15.
11. Luigi Zoja, "Archetypal Backgrounds of Addiction," unpublished lectures, C. G. Jung-Institut, Zurich, January 23 and 24, 1986.
12. Edith Sullwold, "The Ritual-Maker at Adolescence," in *Betwixt and Between,* ed. Louise Carus Mahdi, p. 127.
13. C. G. Jung, *The Symbolic Life,* trans. R.F.C. Hall, vol. 18 of *The Collected Works of C. G. Jung* (Princeton, N.J.: Princeton University Press, 1976), paragraph 653.
14. Robert Kegan, *The Evolving Self: Problem and Process in Human Development* (Cambridge, Mass.: Harvard University Press, 1982), pp. 82, 84.
15. Marina Warner, *Joan of Arc: The Image of Female Heroism* (New York: Vintage Books, 1982).
16. John Knox, *Myth and Truth* (Charlottesville: University Press of Virginia, 1964), p. 29.

17. Paul Ricoeur, "Symbol: Food for Thought," *Philosophy Today* 4 (Spring 1960): 196–207.

18. Campbell, *Hero*, p. 11.

### Chapter 4: Gender and Journey

1. John Sanford, *The Invisible Partners* (New York: Paulist Press, 1980), p. 8.

2. Ibid.

3. Diane Apostolos-Cappadona, "'The Lord has struck him down by the hand of a woman!': Images of Judith," lecture at American Academy of Religion, Boston, December 7, 1987.

4. Copyright Francis B. Rothluebber, *Judith*, Milwaukee, Wis., 1980.

5. For example, see Carol Pearson and Katherine Pope, *The Female Hero in American and British Literature* (New York: Bowker, 1981); and Tristram Potter Coffin, *The Female Hero in Folklore and Legend* (New York: Seabury, 1975).

6. Mara Donaldson, "Woman as Hero in Margaret Atwood's *Surfacing* and Maxine Hong Kingston's *The Woman Warrior*," in *Heroines of Popular Culture*, ed. Pat Browne (Bowling Green, Ohio: Bowling Green State University Popular Press, 1987), pp. 101–13.

7. Demaris S. Wehr, *Jung and Feminism: Liberating Archetypes* (Boston: Beacon Press, 1987), p. 100.

8. Valerie Saiving Goldstein, "The Human Situation: A Feminine Viewpoint," in *The Nature of Man in Theological and Psychological Perspective*, ed. Simon Doniger (New York: Harper & Brothers, 1962), pp. 151–70.

9. Ann Belford Ulanov, *Receiving Woman: Studies in the Psychology and Theology of the Feminine* (Philadelphia: Westminster Press), p. 134.

10. It should be noted that Goldstein also questions any such strict division. In fact, she says that with the increasing feminization of culture, traditional theological estimates of the human condition in respect to categories of sin and redemption may need to be reexamined for both men and women.

11. Carol Pearson, *The Hero Within: Six Archetypes We Live By* (San Francisco: Harper & Row, 1986), pp. 4–9.

12. We are indebted to Peter Hearne of Melbourne, Australia, for this imaginative connection.

### Chapter 5: Understanding Dreams

1. For a discussion of the role of dream handbooks from antiquity on medieval dream literature, see "Macrobius and Medieval Dream Literature," *Medium Ævum* 54 (1985): 59–73. We are indebted to Professor

Raymond Tripp for calling this essay to our attention. See also on the role of dreams in Christian history Morton F. Kelsey's *God, Dreams, and Revelation* (Minneapolis, Minn.: Augsburg, 1968).

### Chapter 6: The Call to Adventure

1. C. S. Lewis, "The Dethronement of Power," in *Tolkien and the Critics*, ed. Neil D. Isaacs and Rose A. Zimbardo (Notre Dame, Ind.: University of Notre Dame Press, 1968), p. 15.
2. John A. Sanford, *The Man Who Wrestled with God* (King of Prussia, Pa.: Religious Pub. Co., 1974), p. 87.
3. Viktor E. Frankl, *Man's Search for Meaning: An Introduction to Logotherapy* (New York: Washington Square Press, 1963), p. 104.
4. C. G. Jung, *The Symbolic Life*, trans. R.F.C. Hull, vol. 18 of *The Complete Works of C. G. Jung* (Princeton, N.J.: Princeton University Press, 1976), paragraphs 257–60.
5. Jung, *Symbols of Transformation*, trans R.F.C. Hull, vol. 5 of *Complete Works*, paragraphs 575–93.

### Chapter 7: Crossing the Threshold

1. Genesis 4:23–24. Scripture quotations are from the Revised Standard Version of the Bible.
2. William Shakespeare, *The Life of King Henry the Fifth*, Act IV, scene iii, lines 22, 64–67.
3. Winston Churchill, *Their Finest Hour* (Boston: Houghton Mifflin, 1949), p. 330.
4. E. V. Gordon, ed., *The Battle of Maldon* (New York: Appleton-Century-Crofts, 1966), lines 312–13. Author's translation.
5. Fr. Klaeber, ed., *Beowulf and the Fight at Finnsburg* (Lexington, Mass.: D. C. Heath, 1922), lines 499–594. Author's translation.
6. Charles W. Kennedy, trans., *An Anthology of Old English Poetry* (New York: Oxford University Press, 1960), p. 24.
7. *The Denver Post*, April 16, 1982, p. 17A.

### Chapter 8: Discernment: Helpers or Tempters

1. Robert Duncan, "My Mother Would Be a Falconress," in *The Norton Anthology of Poetry* (New York: Norton, 1970), pp. 565–66, lines 1–6.
2. John Keats, "La Belle Dame Sans Merci," in *Norton Anthology of Poetry*, pp. 316–17, lines 37–40.
3. Marie-Louise von Franz, *On Divination and Synchronicity: The Psychology of Meaningful Chance* (Toronto: Inner City Books, 1980), p. 77.

4. C. S. Lewis, *The Horse and His Boy* (New York: Macmillan, 1954), pp. 136–40, 155.
5. Joseph Henderson, "Ancient Myths and Modern Man," in *Man and His Symbols*, ed. Carl G. Jung and M.-L. von Franz (Garden City, N.Y.: Doubleday, 1964), pp. 110–12.
6. Roy Wagner, "Totemism," in *The Encyclopedia of Religion*, ed. Mircea Eliade (New York: Macmillan, 1987), 14:573–76.

### Chapter 9: The Road of Trials

1. Bruno Bettelheim, *The Uses of Enchantment* (New York: Knopf, 1977), p. 3.
2. C. G. Jung, *Psychology and Alchemy*, trans. R.F.C. Hull, vol. 12 of *The Collected Works of C. G. Jung* (Princeton, N.J.: Princeton University Press, 1953), paragraph 438.
3. C. G. Jung, *Memories, Dreams, Reflections* (New York: Vintage Books, 1961), pp. 180–81.
4. Anthony Storr, *Jung: Selected Writings* (London: Fontana Paperbacks, 1983), p. 83.

### Chapter 10: Rites of Passage

1. Mircea Eliade, "Initiation: An Overview," in *The Encyclopedia of Religion*, ed. Mircea Eliade (New York: Macmillan, 1987), 7:229.
2. T. S. Eliot, "The Waste Land," in *Collected Poems: 1909–1935* (London: Faber & Faber, 1958), pp. 59–84.
3. Joseph Henderson, "Ancient Myths and Modern Man," in *Man and His Symbols*, ed. Carl G. Jung and M.-L. von Franz (Garden City, N.Y.: Doubleday, 1964), p. 123.
4. Evelyn Eaton Whitehead and James D. Whitehead, *Christian Life Patterns: The Psychological Challenges and Religious Invitations of Adult Life* (Garden City, N.Y.: Doubleday, 1979).
5. Henderson, "Ancient Myths," p. 114.
6. Leonel L. Mitchell, *The Meaning of Ritual*, (New York: Paulist Press, 1977), p. 16.
7. Ibid.

### Chapter 11: The Return

1. Joseph Campbell, *The Hero with a Thousand Faces* (Princeton, N.J.: Princeton University Press, 1949), pp. 29, 28.
2. Alan Sillitoe, *The Loneliness of the Long-Distance Runner* (New York: New American Library, 1959).

3. C. G. Jung, *Symbols of Transformation*, trans. R.F.C. Hull, vol. 5 of *The Complete Works of C. G. Jung* (Princeton, N.J.: Princeton University Press, 1976), paragraph 612.

4. Joseph Henderson, "Ancient Myths and Modern Man," in *Man and His Symbols*, ed. Carl G. Jung and M.-L. von Franz (Garden City, N.Y.: Doubleday, 1964), pp. 110–12.

5. Monica Furlong, *Contemplating Now* (Cambridge, Mass.: Cowley Publications, 1983; rpt, Philadelphia: Westminster Press, 1971), p. 47.

6. Gerald H. Slusser, *From Jung to Jesus: Myth and Consciousness in the New Testament* (Atlanta: John Knox Press, 1986).

7. J. R. R. Tolkien, *The Return of the King, Being the Third Part of the Lord of the Rings* (London: George Allen & Unwin, 1955).

### Chapter 12: Dreams and Suicide

1. Genesis 3:22–24.
2. Numbers 22:21–35.

### Chapter 14: A Monk's Dreams

1. Thomas Merton, *The Asian Journal* (New York: New Directions, 1968), p. 96.
2. John 4:23.
3. Merton, *Asian Journal*, p. 107.
4. Ibid., pp. 324–25.
5. Ibid., pp. 152–53.
6. Ibid., p. 340.
7. Ibid., p. 333.
8. Job 42:5–6.
9. Luke 24:32.

### Chapter 15: A Nun's Dreams

1. For example, C. S. Lewis, *Till We Have Faces* (London: Geoffrey Bles, 1956); Erich Neumann, *Amor and Psyche: The Psychic Development of the Feminine* (New York: Pantheon Books, 1956); Robert A. Johnson, *She: Understanding Feminine Psychology* (New York: Harper & Row, 1977); Jean Shinoda Bolen, *Goddesses in Every Woman: A New Psychology of Women* (San Francisco: Harper & Row, 1984).

2. *The Golden Ass of Apuleius*, trans. Robert Graves (New York: Pocket Books, 1952), pp. 120–27.

3. Neil Canavan, unpublished lecture, Jung Society of Colorado, Denver, October 12, 1984.

4. Robert L. Moore, "Space and Transformation in Human Experience," in *Anthropology and the Study of Religion*, ed. Robert L. Moore and Frank E. Reynolds (Chicago: Center for the Scientific Study of Religion, 1984), pp. 138, 141.

5. C. S. Lewis, *The Lion, the Witch, and the Wardrobe* (New York: Macmillan, 1950).

### Chapter 16: Prayer and Active Imagination

1. *Nana I Ke Kumu (Look to the Source)* (Honolulu: Queen Liliuokalani Children's Center, n.d.), 2:178. For calling our attention to this reference, we are indebted to Sally McDermott of Honolulu, whose husband, John F. McDermott, Jr., M.D., chairman, Department of Psychiatry, John A. Burns School of Medicine, University of Hawaii, consulted on this study of Hawaiian dream lore.

2. S. M. Kamakau, *Ka Poe Kahiko (The People of Old)* (Honolulu: Bishop Museum Press, 1968), p. 73.

3. James A. Michener, *Hawaii* (New York: Random House, 1959), pp. 78–79, 92, 107–8. We are indebted to Anne Clift Boris for calling our attention to this fictional reference to the shark as inner guide.

### Afterword

1. C. G. Jung, *Mysterium Coniunctionis*, trans. R.F.C. Hull, vol. 14 of *The Collected Works of C. G. Jung* (New York: Pantheon Books, 1963), paragraph 756.

2. Laurens van der Post, *The Face Beside the Fire* (London: Hogarth Press, 1953), p. 239.

3. John W. Dixon, Jr., "The Christology of Michelangelo: The Sistine Chapel," *Journal of the American Academy of Religion* 55, no. 3 (1987): 503–33.

4. C. S. Lewis, *The Great Divorce: A Dream* (London: Geoffrey Bles, 1947).

5. Matthew 25:31–46.

6. John Mattern, unpublished lectures at the Seventh Biennial Jungian Winter Seminar, Zurich, Switzerland, January 8 and 9, 1986.

# Index

Acceptance, of unacceptable, 47
Action
   heroic quality of, 39, 40
   lack of, 55
Active imagination, 9, 51, 115
   modes of, 189
   prayer and, 183–190
Advertising, use of symbols in, 26
Affirmation, 82, 87, 116, 168, 188
Alter-ego, 105
American Association of Pastoral Counselors (AAPC), 139, 140
Amor and Psyche (Greek mythology), 174–175
Angel sponsor dream, 79–83
Anger, 55, 56, 71, 169
   dealing with, 164
Animals
   dreams about, 83–89
   in myths and fairy tales, 78
   *See also* Friendly animals, as helpers
Animus/anima figure, 30, 41, 53, 56, 79, 89, 102, 104, 116, 148, 183
   positive, 185
   sources of, 31
Antihero, 127–128
Anxiety, 100, 101, 138

Apostolos-Cappadona, Diane, 32
Archetypes, 34, 37
   snake as, 62
Aristotle, 23
*Asian Journal* (Merton), 165, 170, 177
Assertion, lack of, 100
Attitudes
   changing, 104
   destructive, 57
   father-principle-animus, 133
   negative, 185
   source of, 156
   warlike, 66
*Aumakua* (ancester god), 189
*Australia's Kakadu Man*, 11
Authority, accepting one's, 137, 140
Autopsy, dreams about, 55-58
Awareness, 20, 74, 92, 137
   new challenge of, 104

Baptism, symbols of, 114–115
Baptism of Jesus, 91
*Barrington Bunny*, 86, 89
Bees, dreams about, 146
Behavior, self-limiting, 55
Behavior patterns, 155
   identifying, 5–12

Beowulf, 52, 65
*Betwixt and Between: Patterns of Masculine and Feminine Initiation*, 22
Biblical stories, 16, 61, 91, 150
Blood, as ritual image, 118–119
Bloodletting, 118
Boasts, 63–65
Bolen, Jean, 175
Boredom, 192
Boundaries, setting, 100–103

Call to adventure, 13, 20, 27, 45–60, 122
  exercises for reflection, 196
  reaffirmation of, 152
  realization, 48–49
  refusal of, 58–60, 61
Calvaries, 19
Campbell, Joseph, 13, 17, 20, 22–23, 28, 35, 45, 126
Canavan, Neil, 178
Cancer fears, dream reflecting, 55–58
Car dreams, 73, 86
Caves, dreams about, 103–104
Ceasing to be, 150
Change
  fear of, 68–69
  slow nature of, 161–162
*Chariots of Fire*, 79
Chartres Cathedral, 92
Chicken Little (story character), 7
Child's specialness, exaggeration of, 138–139
Choice(s), 5, 48, 192
  conscious, 6
*Christian Life Patterns: The Psychological Challenges and Religious Invitations of Adult Life* (Whitehead), 109

Churchill, Winston, 64, 65
Closed vessel, 179
Cohesiveness, 94
Collective unconscious, 37–38
Comfort, symbol of, 115
Coming of age, 109–110. *See also* Initiation rituals
Community celebration, 20
Community relationships, failure in, 182
Community rituals, 108
Confession, 24
  ritual dream of, 119–122
Confidence, lack of, 71–72
Conflict, 47, 183
  inner, 89, 164
Conformity, 16
Confusion, 134–137, 175
Consciousness, 7, 8, 92, 131
  coming to, 17
  growth in, 47, 128
  light as symbol of, 46
  and unconsciousness, 9
Consciousness raising, 29
  in women's movement, 30
Courage, 23, 27, 62, 63–66, 79, 159, 186
  building, 66, 67
  ritual forms to build, 67–68
Creation myths, 17
Creativity, primary component, 9
Crops for harvest, dream of, 133–134
Crossing the threshold, 61–75, 156
  dangers in, 98–100
  encouragement in, 69–75
  exercises for reflection, 196
"Cultural promoter" of people, 73
Culture heroes, 18, 27. *See also* Hero(es)
Curiosity, 47

Darkness and confusion, dreams about, 134–137
Death
　dreams about, 147–148, 176
　symbolic, 22
Death-rebirth cycle, 110
Decision making, 98–99. *See also* Choice(s)
Dependency, 151–152
Depression, 160, 161, 173
　examining, 156
　periodic, 155
Devaluation, personal, 83
Discernment, 76–89, 99, 189
Discipline, 82
*Divine Comedy* (Dante), 136, 192
Donaldson, Mara, 33, 34
Donne, John, 193
Dragon figure, 16–17, 163–164, 169
"Dream reentry," 187
Dreams, 4, 23, 126
　animus/anima figures in, 30, 41, 56, 79, 89, 102, 104, 116, 148, 183
　compensatory, 38, 40, 41, 70
　consoling, 72–73
　interpretation of, 37–43
　suicide and, 145–153
　terrifying, 145–153
Dream series, 38
Dream work, two dangers in, 148
Dual parentage, 16

Ego, 33, 192
　connection of, with the Self, 93
　conscious, 183
　identifying with hero, 127
　sacrifice of, 19
　strengthening of, 109
　weak, 86

Ego development, 17
Eliade, Mircea, 21, 108, 179
Elitism, 118
Emotional distance, 175
Emotions, identifying with, 164
Enantiodromia, 7
Encouragement, 73
　from dream helpers, 69–70
　positive, 116–117
Envy, 6
Exclusivity, 118

Fairy tales, 14, 45–56, 126
　common motif in, 78
　unrealistic endings, 20
Family interactions, awareness of, 157–158
Family stories, 10–11
Fear(s), 56, 183
　acknowledging, 84–85
　of being alone, 70–71
Fighting a snake, dreams of, 52–53
Financial issues, dreams about, 94–95
Focus
　lack of, 49
　need of, 175
Foreign country, dreams about, 49–50
Fowler, James, 11
Frankl, Viktor, 48, 57
Freedom, lack of, 54–55
Friendly animals, as helpers, 14, 77–78, 83–84
Frog King (fairy tale), 45–46
*From Jung to Jesus: Myth and Consciousness in the New Testament* (Slusser), 131
Furlong, Monica, 130

Gender, and hero journey, 29–36

General amplification, of dream symbols, 38, 118, 154, 189
Gentle spirit, 78, 79
God imagery, 130, 152, 168, 171
Goldstein, Valerie Saiving, 33
Grandiosity, 139
*Great Divorce, The* (Lewis), 192
Grief, 72
Guilt, 188

Hall, James, 19
Halliburton, Richard, adventures of, 9
Hanuman (hero-god), 165
*Hawaii* (Michener), 189
Healing, need for, 172
Healing ritual, 115–117
Hebrew Scripture, stories from, 62–63
Helpers, 76–89, 164, 192
　animal, 77–78, 83–84, 181
　anonymous, 157
　encouragement from, 69–70
　exercises for reflection, 196–197
　super-power, 110
　trickster, 165
Helplessness, 83
　and authority, contrast between, 104
Henderson, Joseph, 22, 109, 128
Henry V (king), 64, 65
Hercules, 52, 94
Hero(es)
　absolute, 17
　attitude toward word, 17
　birth of, 16
　as changed person, 129
　female, 32–36
　gender-free usage, 29
　sacrifice of, 92
　weakness in, 88
Hero journey

call to adventure, 45–60
　dangerous aspect of, 78
　failed, 128
　fear of, 151
　goal of, 130
　linear and circular aspects of, 35
　pain in, 141, 175, 176
　perilous, 151–153
　the return, 126–141
　road of trials, 90–107
　typology of, 34
Hero myth, 22. *See also* Myths; Story(ies)
Hero stories, individuality in, 34
*Hero with a Thousand Faces, The* (Campbell), 13
Historical characters, dreams about, 39–40
Historical stories, 64–65
*Horse and His Boy, The*, 83
Hubris, 33, 34, 127, 140, 188
Human development, 18
　love as ultimate goal, 130
　psychological significance of gender in, 30–31
　slow nature of, 161–162
Human journey, 21–28
Humility, 33, 34, 59, 137
"Hundredth monkey phenomenon," 128

Idolatry, 129
*Image and Pilgrimage in Christian Culture: Anthropological Perspectives* (Turner), 22
Images
　associations with, 4, 37
　contrasexual, 30
　positive, 158
　religious, 169, 170
　spiritual, 147
Inadequacy, 138, 184

Individuality, 26–27, 34, 35
Individuation process, 19, 33, 89, 92, 109, 191
Initiation, 14, 21
Initiation rite (ritual), 22–27, 108–109
　and hero myth, distinction between, 22
Inner development, 47
Inner voice. *See* Consciousness
Innocence, 79
Intensive Journal Workshops, 9
Intuition rituals, 26
*Invisible Partners, The* (Sanford), 31

Jesus, 18, 61, 63, 129, 130–131, 170, 188, 189
　as "master of two worlds," 131
Joan of Arc, 27, 39, 180
Johnson, Robert, 175
Jonah (biblical character), 18, 91
Journaling, 9–10, 118
Judas (disciple), 76–77
*Judith* (cantata), 32
Jung, C. G., 3, 4, 7, 8, 17, 19, 25, 30–31, 33, 37, 52, 91, 92, 121, 130, 149, 161, 168, 178, 179, 191

Kegan, Robert, 26
*King Lear*, 79
Knox, John, 28

"La Belle Dame Sans Merci" (Keats), 78
Leadership, dreams about, 95–97
L'Engle, Madeleine, 86
Lewis, C. S., 47
Life
　growth as evidence of, 109
　newness of, 115
Liminality, 21–22

*Lion, the Witch, and the Wardrobe, The* (Lewis), 181
*Little Engine That Could, The*, 6
"Little Red Hen," 5
Logotherapy, 48
Loneliness, 70–71, 98, 99
*Loneliness of the Long Distance Runner* (Sillitoe), 127
*Lord of the Rings, The*, 137

Mahdi, Louise Carus, 22
Manic-depressive personality type, 8
Marriage, 20, 23, 24, 41
Mattern, John, 192
May, Rollo, 4
Meaning-making process, 26
Merton, Thomas, 165, 170
Midlife crisis, 109
Mikvah, 112
Mitchell, Leonel, 112
Mohammed Ali, 67
Monastic therapy, 172
Monk's dream, 163–172
Monomyth, 13–20, 33, 38, 192
　building up courage, 68
　departure, 13–14
　initiation, 14
　return threshold, 14
Moore, Robert L., 178
Moral failure, 129
Morality, 4
Moses, 16, 18, 47–48
Mutilation, dreams about, 98–100, 147–148, 176
"My Mother Would Be a Falconress" (Duncan), 77
*Myth of the Birth of the Hero* (Rank), 16
Myths, 4, 126
　emotional response to, 23
　myriad forms, 19

National Conference of Christians and Jews (1981), 32
Nazis, dreams about, 117–119
Neanderthal men, dreams about, 73–75
Nebuchadnezzar, 62
Neumann, Erich, 19, 175
Neurosis, 17, 140
*Never Cry Wolf,* 86
No, learning to say, 175
Nun's dream, 173–182

O'Connor, Flannery, 17
Olivier, Laurence, 64
Oneness, transcendent vision of, 171
Openness, 79
Orderliness, 82
Ordination, ritual dream of, 122–125, 184

Pain
  dreams about, 175, 176
  hiding from, 161
"Parting of the Red Sea, The," 66
Pearson, Carol, 34
Personal amplification, of dream symbols, 37, 40, 154
Personal growth, 118
Personality
  anima/animus figure role and, 30
  extravert-intuitive, 7
  introvert, 9
  manic-depressive, 8
  reintegration of, 178
Pilgrimage, 22, 28
Pius X, Saint, 123, 124
*Places of the Heart,* 48
Power
  accepting one's, 137
  assimilation of, 175
  overidentifying with, 140
  positive image of, 57
Prayer, and active imagination, 183–190
Primordial patterns of human behavior, 37
Progoff, Ira, 9, 10, 169
Projection, 92
  idealized, 139
Psychic energy flow, 31
Purification, 92, 110–114

Racial stories, 11
Rebirth, 130, 180
  symbolic, 22
Reconciliation, 20, 130
  of unknown, 136
Reflection, 8–9, 16
Relationships
  loss of, 51
  shifting, 152
Religious community stories, 11
Religious rituals, 108. *See also* Ritual(s)
Religious tradition, 62–63
  ceremonies of, 24–25
Reluctant hero, 47
Resentment, 5, 6, 72
Restlessness, 59
Return (from hero journey), 127–142
  difficulty of, 129
  exercises for reflection, 198
  refusal of, 128
Ricoeur, Paul, 28
Risk-taking, 79
Rite of reconciliation. *See* Confession
Rites of passage, 23–24, 108–125
  baptism, 114–115
  coming of age, 109–110

exercises for reflection, 196
primitive, 24
purification, 110–114
*Rites of Passage, The* (van Gennep), 21
Ritual(s), 108, 184
  initiation, 21–27, 108–109
Road of trials, 14, 90–107
  defining boundaries, 100–103
  exercises for reflection, 197
*Roots*, 11

Sacred space, 179
Sacrifice, 19, 22, 117–119
Sandner, Donald, 20
Sanford, John, 47
Security, sense of, 88–89, 105
Self, 30, 70, 168, 192
  avoiding the, 34
  Christ as archetypal image of, 130
  image of, 124
  soul's journey toward, 174–175
  temenos as symbol of, 178
  women's refusal of, 33
Self-acceptance, 117, 138
Self-abasement, 139
Self-affirmation, 33, 34
Self-assertion, 33
Self-esteem
  limitations, 97
  low, 138
Self-examination, 159
Selflessness, 33
Self-understanding, 20
Separation from the father, 110
Separation from the mother, 50–54
Sexuality
  as cause of inner conflict, 111–14
  dealing with, 164
  reexamining attitude towards, 185

"Shadow couple," 41
Shadow figure, 79, 82, 133, 155, 157, 179
  accepting, 135
  assimilation with, 91
  befriending, 136
  confrontation and assimilation of, 109
  positive, 138
Sharing with others, 129, 185
Shark *(mano)* symbol, 189
Sin, 33
Snakes, dreams about, 103–104, 149–150
Social action, 118, 131, 135
Spiritual growth, 18, 22, 128
  change of attitude and, 23
  culture and, 26
Sports stories, 67
*Star Wars*, 48
Storr, Anthony, 92
Story(ies)
  crucial role of, 3
  exercises for reflection, 195–196
  psychological significance, 8–9
  recognition of universal patterns in, 131
  relation of to human lives, 3–12
  *See also* specific type e.g. Biblical stories
Strength, trial of, 91
Sullwold, Edith, 25
Suicide, 102
  dreams and, 145–153
Sundance (Sioux initiation ceremony), 51
Superiority, 118
Suppression, of feelings, 161
Symbolism, 26, 103–104, 119
  religious, 163–172
  *See also* Symbols

Symbols, 24
  as bridge between two realities, 129
  keeping translucent, 130
  power of on unconscious level, 26
  repeated, 154–162
*Symbols of Transformation in Dreams*, 38, 41, 183
Symbol system, living in, 28
Synchronicity, 88, 122, 125

Taunts, 63–65
Teenage suicides, 25
Temenos, 178, 179
Tempters
  exercises for reflection, 196–197
Terror, 192
Tests and tasks, 14, 90
  multiplicity of, 90–107
Therapeutic space, 179
*Thresholds of Initiation* (Henderson), 22
Torture dreams, 140–141
Totemism, 88
Tragedy, 23, 48
Transformation, 18, 19, 108, 149
  space and, 179
Transition moments in life. *See* Rites of passage
Tribal stories, 11
Turner, Victor, 21, 22, 179

Ulanov, Ann, 33
Unconscious, the, 27, 52, 92, 154
  three paths to knowledge of, 4
Understanding, 16
Unknown
  frightening quality of, 41
  perilous journey into, 92
  reconciliation of, 136
*Uses of Enchantment, The* (Bettelheim), 90

Value system, strengthening of, 127
van der Post, Laurens, 12, 191
Violence, dreams of, 176
Visitations, true meaning of, 168
Vocation, 27, 33, 124
  commitment to, 173
  signs of, 14
  summons. *See* Call to adventure
von Franz, Marie-Louise, 78

War, dreams of, 176
War Memorial Museum (Auckland, New Zealand), 67
Warner, Marina, 27
"Waste Land, The" (Eliot), 108
Water, as dream symbol, 112, 146, 154–162
Wayne, John, dreams about, 105–106
Wedding, dreams about, 132–133
Wehr, Demaris, 33
Wholeness, 20, 47, 70, 71
  cross as symbol of, 113
  images of, 30
  social action on, 131
Wisdom, 19, 105, 168
  growth of, 18
*Wizard of Oz*, 48, 77

Yang and Yin, 31

Zoja, Luigi, 25